Rhetorical Agency

Rhetorical Agency

Mind, Meshwork, Materiality, Mobility

Les Belikian

punctum books ⓟ **earth, milky way**

RHETORICAL AGENCY: MIND, MESHWORK, MATERIALITY, MOBILITY
© Les Belikian, 2017.

http://creativecommons.org/licenses/by-nc-sa/4.0/

This work carries a Creative Commons BY-NC-SA 4.0 International license, which means that you are free to copy and redistribute the material in any medium or format, and you may also remix, transform and build upon the material, as long as you clearly attribute the work to the authors (but not in a way that suggests the authors or punctum endorses you and your work), you do not use this work for commercial gain in any form whatsoever, and that for any remixing and transformation, you distribute your rebuild under the same license.

Book design: Mike Smith
Cover design: Eileen A. Joy

First published in 2017 by
punctum books
Earth, Milky Way
https://punctumbooks.com

LCCN: 2017956682
Library of Congress Cataloging Data is available from the Library of Congress.

ISBN-13: 978-1-947447-24-0 (print)
ISBN-13: 978-1-947447-25-7 (ePDF)

HIC SVNT MONSTRA

Before you start to read this book, take this moment to think about making a donation to punctum books, an independent non-profit press,

@ https://punctumbooks.com/support/

If you're reading the e-book, you can click on the image below to go directly to our donations site. Any amount, no matter the size, is appreciated and will help us to keep our ship of fools afloat. Contributions from dedicated readers will also help us to keep our commons open and to cultivate new work that can't find a welcoming port elsewhere.

Vive la Open Access.

Fig. 1. Hieronymus Bosch, *Ship of Fools* (1490-1500)

for Nevart Mary Knivett

TABLE OF CONTENTS

// i

Preface.

// 1

Chapter 1. Productivity as a Context for Theorizing Rhetorical Transaction • A Miscellaneously Self-Effacing Rhetorical Agency? • Rhetoricity Bound, Unbounded, and Both • Variegation (Not Conglomeration)

// 23

Chapter 2. A Four-Folded Rhetorical Agency • Tetradic Due Diligence • Disaggregating a Constitution • A Willfully Productive Rhetorical Agency • Assemblage–Theoretical Resources • Triangulation • An Investigative Itinerary

// 49

Chapter 3. Subjectivity in the Social-Structural Landscape • Co-Constructing Constraint • Can the Speaker Speak? • An Ineffectual Agency • Subtracting from Rhetorical Practice • What Else Is Wrong with This Paradigm? • A Chimerical Agency for a Colossal Agent

// 73

Chapter 4. Conventionality in the Rhetorical-Humanistic Landscape • De-Leviathanizing the Normative • From Normativity to Shared Values • A Tribe of Equals • Keeping Shared Values between the Ceiling and the Seat • Staying the Same by Doing Something Differently • Maximizing Assent by Minimizing Recalcitrance • Still Missing So Far

// 99

Chapter 5. Transcendence in the Existential-Transversal Landscape • Existence, Transcendence, and Transversality • Philosophizing for the Living by Getting Rid of Their Materiality • The Two Styles of Transcendence • The Fideistic Appeal • Correcting Forgetfulness through a Material Phenomenology • Rhetorical Agency and the Existential Self • On Pivoting, Transcendence, and Emergence • The Rhetorical Agent and the Original Body • A Re-Corporealized Transversality

// 129

Chapter 6. Materiality in the Material-Semiotic Landscape • A Parable of Materiality-and-Relationality • Assemblaging, Stratification, and Circulating Reference • Entering at Biblical Precept • Crossing over to Race • From Race to Gender • Rescaling the Envoy • And A'n't We a Meshwork?

// 159

Chapter 7. Agency in the Rhetorical-Theoretical World • No More Homogenization Now! • On Keeping Difference Different • A Fluctuating Rhetorical Agent

// 169

Works Cited.

ACKNOWLEDGMENTS

In a work describing rhetorical agency as multiple, it's appropriate to begin with thanks to those allies whose influences (sometimes oblique, sometimes countervailing) have contributed to making even the beginning possible. They include family members: Sylvia, Jenny, Pearl, Walter, and Pokie Dog. They include colleagues, friends, and students: Ben Attias, Helen Bunn, Galust Mardirussian, Ralph Pililian, Joseph Soltis, Kathryn Sorrells, Fleur Steinhardt, and Konrad Wilk. They include Eileen Joy and Mike Smith at punctum books, together with the anonymous reviewers whose feedback has so strongly shaped the results. They include, though in a manner circuitous indeed, Clay Spinuzzi at the University of Texas at Austin and Mikael M. Karlsson at the University of Iceland. Most of all, they include Peter Marston at California State University, Northridge, without whose insightful pragmatism and patient engagement the project would never have arrived at its form. Yet rhetorical agency is capacious, with room for the individual as well as for the collective. In accepting responsibility for every error, misstep, infelicity still included, I recognize each to be my own.

Preface

IF THE UPCOMING CHAPTERS ever imply any camouflaging of the authorial persona, that impression may simply derive from the humility at stake in arranging for collisions among the perspectives of others. But I'm in the neighborhood anyway, so I'll introduce the work as a whole by previewing the places where the main topics and lines of reasoning are located. (Let me add from the outset, though, that I'm breaking with tradition by previewing the places slightly out of order.) In the process, I'll contribute a few autobiographical anecdotes, each connected with an insight about rhetorical agency. These little stories, just the four of them, might serve as bridges between my sense of the situation and yours. They might also model some of the applications that I hope will come to mind in the rest of the discussion, where rhetorical agency as it works for the theorist meets rhetorical agency as it works for the practitioner.

When theory does refer to "rhetorical agency," the focus generally falls upon the respect in which communication might involve agents who act — instead of patients, as it were, that are passively moved upon. And then a question arises as to what rhetoric might contain (or unleash) that empowers its users to cooperate in action. It's an important question, though it most often gets a quarter-hearted, not even full-throated reply. For rhetoric is credited, and that's about the size of it, with enigmatically managing, or activating, or supervening upon the most crucial of the forces, or capacities, or proclivities which travel along with writing and reading, with speaking and listening, with teaching and learning — with communicative production and reception. So Chapter 1 frames the important question itself as a problem of productivity.

As for the answer to the question, at least the answer uncovered during the present investigation, it's translucent enough to state in a sentence but four-folded enough to explain at length: Rhetorical agency is an assemblage made out of subjectivity, conventionality, materiality, and transcendence, each of which is still under construction. Chapter 2 therefore lays out the essentials of the answer, all of them in the same spot. That's not to say there's nary an air-bubble in the answer. To the contrary, there's a glitch meandering all the way through it, and this is that almost everybody studying rhetorical functionality is currently positioned to discern only one of the components, only one of the constituents of rhetorical agency at a time.

But that reminds me of when I went to see the dentist, the one who asked how Barack Obama's speaking style could ever have gotten the guy elected president. Temporarily supine, familiar with enough of those horror movies to know the drill, I plumped for diplomacy. Why, said I, the explanation had surprisingly little to do with speaking style. It was just that Obama, by invoking certain recurrent ideals, virtues, and aspirations (and this is where I remembered to emphasize not only hope but also change) had managed to create the requisite identification between himself and the public.

Later on, speeding from the scene, I congratulated myself for producing, and under such unnerving conditions, the irrefragable response. For mine had been the sort of reply, give or take, that ought to meet the approval, or so I decided, of contemporary rhetorical theorists such as anybody. Yes, Barack Obama had proven himself to be an agent, and he had done so by invoking certain recurrent ideals, virtues, and aspirations, and my dentist had not demurred.

Surely, as many a recent textbook on argumentation or public speaking would confirm (in a section, say, on the place of "warrants" in the Toulmin model), rhetoric operates not so much, if at all, through eloquence as through leveraging those hoary, durable values which the recipients of a message share with the sender. For what else, if not guidelines held (or, better yet, guidelines valorized) in common could explain why, periodically tabling our atomistic selfishness, we accede to the collective, if still worthy-of-us endeavor? From this perspective, rhetorical agents do not possess any rhetorical agency, certainly not as their private property. They share it with those others in the community who happen to share the same values.

So I've continued researching that entire way of thinking, a line of reasoning which remains every bit as true, as ready-to-hand, and — frankly — as mobile as an Arctic icescape. The results are featured not exactly where you'd expect, but somewhat further along, in Chapter 4. They are (re)visited wherever the text mentions the rhetorical-humanistic perspective, according to which rhetorical agency inheres in conventionality.

Yet there was that other occasion when, eavesdropping upon the conversation between a couple of graduate students, I grasped with some finality that the irrefragable response was not what it used to be. The discussion was about the Mexican-born Selma Hayek, topical for having so recently received U.S. citizenship. And what difference would switching passports make for a celebrity of that stature? Would it alter her talent as a performer, her ability as a director — would it modify her financial wherewithal, her engagement as a political activist? No, but it would still increase her "agency."

If that were the case, or so I began to suspect, then one could probably factor out the appeal of any shared values expressed in Salma Hayek's performances, projects, or platforms, since the shared values themselves would remain equally appealing regardless of Salma Hayek's nationality. But then the numerator, or what accounted for this upgrade in Salma Hayek's agency, would be the hegemonic power with which Salma Hayek had just now become identified.

In other words, these graduate students, here reduced to anonymity but still shepherded along by their up-to-date reading assignments, had every reason to conclude that agency accrued not so much, if at all, to shared values as to the control mechanisms locking down the group. Remembering the dentist's office, remembering Barack Obama (remembering, that is, a rhetorical situation lined with X-ray images, with testimonials to expertise), I realized that what the graduate students were saying — that agency belongs to the state — was, regrettably, correct. From this perspective, rhetorical agents neither possess nor share any rhetorical agency: they lease as much of it as allowed to by law.

So I've continued researching that entire way of thinking, a line of reasoning which remains every bit as true and conflictual as a traffic ticket. The results are featured back there in Chapter 3 and (re)visited wherever the text mentions the social-structural perspective, according to which rhetorical agency inheres in subjectivity.

Then a certain communication instructor briefly contracted the flu, which briefly became associated with pneumonia, which briefly resulted in hospitalization. There were doctors, nurses, visitors, medical assistants, some of whom, dropping by to maintain the IV drip stuck into a left arm, might have observed the tapping out, with a right hand, of e-mail messages to persons.

But where oh where was my rhetorical agency then? It wasn't located so much, if at all, in a set of shared values or ideological pronouncements as in a relational-yet-tangible mesh. That alliance, so far as I could tell, included not only all of the preceding but also quite a few buildings, pillows, forms of medical knowledge, students, healthcare systems, sensations, pieces of specialized equipment, affiliations and livelihoods, sheets, perceptions, viruses and germs, interests and agendas, ideas for thesis statements.

In short, what must be accurate to say of agency (and, while we're at it, of patiency too) is that it's distributed irreducibly among all sorts of actors pulling together, regardless that most of them aren't even human. From this perspective, rhetorical agents neither possess, nor share, nor yet lease any rhetorical agency. They emerge, together with rhetorical agency, as network effects.

So I've continued researching that entire way of thinking, a line of reasoning which remains every bit as true and internally heterogeneous as an alloy. The results are featured all the way over in Chapter 6. They are (re)visited wherever the text mentions the material-semiotic perspective, according to which rhetorical agency inheres in materiality, albeit the kind of materiality that's relational as well as tangible.

Nevertheless, lying as I was in my hospital bed (though that's an allusion both to Bo Diddley and to the New York

Dolls), I kept registering that the typing hand, the one tapping out those e-mail messages to persons, wasn't somebody else's. No doubt the abstract-and-concrete totality did seem more real than it ought to be. But to the extent that it existed, then it existed, if at all, not so much for better or worse as for me. There's undeniably something for each of us, isn't there, in Sarah McLachlan's "Fumbling Towards Ecstasy": "It's my heart that pounds beneath my flesh / It's my mouth that pushes out this breath." From this perspective, rhetorical agents neither possess, nor share, nor lease, nor yet sit around waiting for the emergence of any rhetorical agency. They stake a claim to rhetorical agency despite their enmeshment in the network.

So I've continued researching that entire way of thinking, a line of reasoning which remains every bit as true and (shucks) improbable as your presence. The results are featured in the place that's been missing so far — namely, Chapter 5 — and they are (re)visited wherever the text mentions the existential-transversal perspective, according to which agency inheres in transcendence.

Those little anecdotes, all four of them, might yet become bridges and models, entrances into the study of a four-folded rhetorical agency. Chapter 7, the conclusion, even offers a suggestion for bridging the models, but without effacing the boundaries among them. As to whether theory takes the hint, that's hardly for me to say.

1.
Productivity as a Context for Theorizing Rhetorical Transaction

IN THE FOLLOWING STUDY, applying an assemblage-theoretical approach to a canonical text, we'll investigate the prospects for conceptualizing rhetorical agency as the enactment — the production — of social change. Certainly, rhetorical agency is often studied as a potential, a capacity first held in reserve by speakers and listeners and then, in principle, brought to bear during rhetorical transaction (see Campbell or Herndl and Licona). Yet it's important to theorize rhetorical agency as a kinetic manifestation, not just as a possible supply of communicative energies. Doing so would justify our seeking rhetoric's effectivity, our circumventing the suspicion that communication might only be to mirror the conditions already in place.

Is it possible conceptually to link rhetorical functionality with social change? It ought to be. While definitions of "rhetoric" abound, the most familiar must be that furnished by Aristotle, describing rhetoric as an ability to find the available means of persuasion, and thereby affirming that rhetoric's very rationale is to create change. Elsewhere in the *Rhetoric*, Aristotle adds that "most of the matters with which judgments and examination are concerned can be other than they are, for people deliberate and examine what they are doing, and [human] actions are all of this kind" (*Aristotle: On Rhetoric* 42). Similarly, in the *Nichomachean Ethics*, he portrays "the deliberative faculty" itself as that through which we engage "things that are variable" — not things that simply "move," but "things that in their very being can be otherwise than they are" (McNeill 32).

Today, we are all the more inclined to view social relations as among these variable, contingent things, these matters which, through deliberation and other forms of collective enterprise, can be made otherwise than they are. In that case, it should indeed be possible conceptually to link rhetoric with social change, and even to demonstrate how the former could produce the latter.

However, an array of theorists have come to deprecate the Aristotelian model as instrumentalist, as attributing to rhetorical utterance the causal efficacy of some philosophical slingshot. Commentators have even discerned in that framework a "primeval elitism," the ascription, to certain special speakers, of an uncommon will to suasion, an inherent ability to galvanize such audiences as would prefer to remain inert (McGee 22). To be sure, not everyone in rhetorical studies has found the Aristotelian view so exceptionable. It does, after all, situate the audience as "more than a target, more than a consumer," indeed, as "a kind of collaborative agency for making ongoing judgments" (Farrell 96). Still, rhetorical theory has persistently developed strategies for exiting from instrumentalism—each of them, come to think of it, according less and less agency to the human actors who would have to operationalize any genuine social change.

By now, those alternative means of escape have evidently allowed researchers to depart from an outworn "logic of influence," this latter being the allegation that rhetoric can "modify attitudes or induce action on the part of consummate individuals" (Biesecker 232). Thus the successors to the Aristotelian position (that cornerstone of the traditional stance) have outstripped both the notion that rhetoric might express the resistless will of the rhetor, and the notion that rhetoric might stage-manage the thoughts and behaviors of subjects imagined as stable, fully formed, self-sufficient. Even so, the counter-Aristotelian approaches have not abolished every last trace of instrumentalism, causality, or influence, for they have not left us with a vision of rhetoric as contributing nothing. Instead, as an overview of the last quarter-century's worth of rhetorical-theoretical development could show, each of them has merely displaced the locus of rhetorical effectivity.

For, although there have been shifts in the characterization of the properly rhetorical mode, rhetorical effectivity is still located somewhere. Clearly, it's no longer located, not exclusively so, at the instrumentalist site of a purposively collaborative intentionality, or at the epistemic site of intra-collective knowledge, or at the critical-constitutive site of interpellative expression, or at the just plain constitutive site of self-regenerating symbolization, or at the articulatory site where "this practice" is linked unobtrusively "to that effect, this text to that meaning, this meaning to that reality" (Grossberg qtd. in Greene, *Another*, 34–35). Instead, rhetorical effectivity is apparently located at all of these sites, the lot of them inhering within what some commentators might go so far as to call the social totality.

If we were to reflect on these contemporary viewpoints on rhetorical functionality, all of them involving the (often occluded) assumption that rhetoric does retain some effectivity, we would see that they turn out, without exception, to share an emphasis on rhetoric as *productive*, whether or not that label is highlighted in their description. Therefore the point remains that, so long as there's rhetorical effectivity (so long as rhetoric is, indeed, productive), we really oughtn't to have much difficulty finding a theoretical justification for linking rhetoric (say, by way of collective action) with genuine social change.

Unfortunately, rhetoric nowadays is not only epistemic, duplicitous, constitutive, and articulatory, but also woven into an autopoetic social logic, a collective trajectory within which speakers and listeners are caught up, but over which they have precious little say. Our own project, therefore, will be to help repopulate rhetorical transaction by locating precisely the sort of agency through which rhetoricity could articulate with social change. The contribution here will be to lay out, in contrast to much of the rhetorical-theoretical common sense about such matters, a conceptual argument designed to upset some widespread notions as to rhetoric's productivity, and, more specifically, to counteract an otherwise unfettered trend to diminish the role of any human actors. Yet the point of our diverging from that trend isn't to bypass the study of agency as practiced within contemporary rhetorical scholarship, nor is it to demolish the most salient of the stances already taken. Instead, it's to protect those positions in their own terms, merely reworking their disclosures so as to arrive at a solution.

We should begin by sizing up the problem which the solution is to engage. It's that research has arrived at an impasse such that all the different conceptualizations of rhetorical functionality are, in effect, colluding to undo the agency they ought to be uncovering. That's because not even the theorists of an epistemic, critical, constitutive, and/or articulatory rhetoric can, at present, offer a cogent account of the manner in which rhetoric would indeed link with social change.

A Miscellaneously Self-Effacing Rhetorical Agency?

To explain rhetoric's effectivity in keeping with the accounts provided by contemporary theorists is quite a task. Many such commentators, it's only fair to add, would object that, but of course, the whole purpose of their theorizing is to "reestablish the primacy of rhetorical agency," the reestablishment of this primacy being prerequisite to any arguments about what rhetorical agency might be able to accomplish (Gardner 203). So, to rescale the objection, to bring it down to size, let's note that rhetorical theory has, at present, surprisingly little wherewithal for actually reestablishing the primacy of rhetorical agency. And let's even attempt a glancing survey of the lexicon, the idiom, in which contemporary theorists are talking about the sorts of agency at stake in rhetorical transaction. That way, we ought to be able to see that the salient conceptual vocabulary militates *against* the claim that there's any agency proper to rhetoric to begin with.

Citing Ahern, citing Geisler, citing O'Hair et al., citing Turnbull, citing Campbell, and citing Koerber, Amanda Young (2008) notes that, while rhetorical agency remains "key to rhetorical inquiry," its definition looks, all of a sudden, to be inordinately "slippery and fluid" (227). Christine J. Gardner (2011) concurs. She adds that, even if rhetorical agency does involve "the capacity to act," recent scholars have defined "this slippery term," rhetorical agency, in a "variety of ways" (203). The variety reflects a hydra-headed effort at rehabilitating rhetoric in the face of "a postmodern critique" that, decentering the subject as traditionally conceived, all but "reduces rhetors" to "points of articulation" (Gardner 203). So, although rhetorical agency can't nowadays be treated as the province of a sovereign subject, it can at least be studied as *ideology*, or as *power*, or as *responsibility*, or — perhaps a bit disingenuously — as *human potential*, or as *resource*, or as *performance*, or as *illusion*, all of these emerging as equally acceptable definitions (Gardner 203).

No wonder Amanda Young would take such care to emphasize that, when it comes to talk of rhetorical agency, "the challenge is not simply" to define it, but "to recognize it in context," the implication being that each definition, in stipulating its own preferred context, will dictate which sorts of evidentiary claims may be admitted in the first place (228). But this must be why rhetorical agency is so slippery and fluid: it's everything from the quintessentially ideological and the authentically responsible to the inherently performative and the merely illusory. Remarkably, though — as Young further explains, drawing on pieces by Turnbull, by Young and Flower, by Flower, by Koerber, by O'Hair et al., and by Campbell — rhetorical agency has also managed to acquire certain "fundamental properties," and these include *questioning, negotiation, choice*, and *evaluation* (228).

The conundrum, then, is that rhetorical agency is currently being conceptualized in a manner that precludes any reestablishment of its primacy, since this is an agency whose own contents, ranging from "choice" to "ideology" — opposites as these are — must forever be undertaking a sort of mutual effacement. To pursue the point a little further, if only for the sake of clarity, let's consider what happens to rhetorical agency when it's conceptualized in terms not only of "ideology" but also of "choice." For this amounts to theory's giving with one hand while taking away with the other, as by devising a view in which rhetorical agency is nebulously deterministic, but, then again, nebulously voluntaristic, too.

Rhetoricity Bound, Unbounded, and Both

If we could try to keep "ideology" and "choice" apart for just a heuristic moment, then "ideology," pure and simple, would refer to a framework (for our thought and action) which is quintessentially directive, justificatory, comprehensive or totalistic in tendency, and unconscious. By contrast, "choice," pure and simple, would imply our ability willfully to opt out of any framework whatever, no matter how directive and totalistic that framework might be. But the definition of "ideology" contradicts the definition of "choice," just as the definition of "choice" contradicts the definition of "ideology." And even if choice really is a "fundamental property" of rhetorical agency, there's no self-evident method for distinguishing between, on the one side, a determined, ideological modality of choice and, on the other side, an untrammeled, voluntaristic modality of choice (Young 228). Therefore, a rhetorical agency in which "ideology" is theoretically sutured to "choice" must be next to useless, for the reason that it is too voluntaristic to be tenable, and yet too deterministic to make any difference.

To be sure, many of us would hew to the position that even ideology can't be seamless, that it necessarily betrays internal fissures. As Christian O. Lundberg (2009) asks, in rejoinder to Ronald Walter Greene, what about "failed interpellations," and what about "impotence in the governing apparatus?" (183). But the question as to interpellative failure and/or managerial incompetence is still separate from the question as to choice. For choice, pure and simple, would be sometimes to choose against competent and even successful interpellations. Therefore "choice" remains tied to voluntarism, whereas "ideology" (successful, incompetent, or whatever) remains tied to determinism instead. At the same time, so long as rhetoricity is promiscuously distributed between an improbable determinism and an unworkable voluntarism, then to say that its agency equates to "human potential" is to say nothing about it at all (Gardner 203).

If we were in a position to recognize whether it's the deterministically ideological that trumps the voluntaristically chosen, or whether it's the other way around, then we would be able to decide whether rhetorical transaction can make things otherwise than they are. But not only are we not in any such position, we are not even in a position to rule, other than by resorting to theoretical fiat, on so much as the difference between the ideological and the chosen. For, on the one side, there's the never-ending regress of the ideological, to which theorists can retreat against the threat of voluntarism, and, on the other side, there's the never-ending regress of the chosen, to which theorists can retreat against the threat of determinism. The only way out of either regress would be to make a flat-out assertion, as by saying "Yes, determinism trumps voluntarism, or "Yes, voluntarism flouts determinism," or, alternatively, "Yes, both determinism and voluntarism are just as irreducible as can be."

As for the question of consensus, well, according to Christine J. Gardner and others (see, for example, Lundberg and Gunn 102), the best that contemporary rhetorical theory has to offer in the way of a leading indication, in the way of a statement that evokes "the essence of the plurality of views," must be Karlyn Kohrs Campbell's celebrated argument of 2005, an argument in which rhetorical agency is disclosed as promiscuous, protean, perverse, and even paradoxical (Gardner 203). Indeed, if research into agency is travel, then Campbell's "Agency: Promiscuous and Protean" has become a must-see attraction, highlighted as such in a substantive, even sumptuous brochure titled *The Sage Handbook of Rhetorical Studies* (2009), edited by Lunsford, Wilson, and Eberly. That reference work begins with a series of "road-maps" for the student of rhetoric, one of them explaining exactly where to look for "Rhetorical Agents and Agency" (xxi–xxiv). Many individual studies are cited there, though in a manner not so much economical as abstemious. It's only in the case of Campbell's text that the editors include entire paragraphs, one after the other. And this must be to leave no doubt that, no matter how many miscellaneous treatments there may be to choose from, Campbell's "Agency: Promiscuous and Protean" is, for the foreseeable future, pretty much the last word on this slippery and fluid topic.

But if rhetorical agency can really be as miscellaneous as Campbell indicates, then it will have to be not only slippery and fluid but homogeneous as well. It will have to populate the black box of rhetorical transaction with, for example, "power" as indistinguishable from "illusion," and with "ideology" as coextensive with "choice," all of these inhering, precisely as theorized in contemporary rhetorical studies, in one and the same rhetorical agency. Meanwhile, any rhetorical agency conceptualized in this way will forever be canceling itself out. For, under a description of rhetorical agency as so interminably miscellaneous, whatever is (for example) authentically and voluntaristically progressive about rhetorical agency can, in theory, also prove to be whatever is treacherous, deterministic, and retrogressive about rhetorical agency. The problem becomes that, so long as rhetorical agency is all things to all rhetorical theorists, it's just too plain fluid and promiscuous to help us establish any intelligible connection between rhetorical functionality and genuine social change.

Variegation (Not Conglomeration)

We do seem presented with a conception of rhetorical agency as, on the one side, surprisingly complicated (for this is an agency that can collocate everything from hard-core power to solipsistic illusion) and yet, on the other side, astonishingly simple (for this very same agency is not just sometimes but always elusive). Still, to the extent that the line of reasoning pursued by Campbell does remain helpful, then we should embrace the possibilities it discloses. Indeed, the internal structure of Campbell's own argument suggests an expedient for simplifying the busyness, and yet for complicating the single-mindedness, that attends the present-day theorization of rhetorical agency. For, even as "Agency: Protean and Promiscuous" implies that rhetorical agency must always be undoing itself, it also implies that rhetorical agency must always be proceeding from *somewhere* — and not just from anywhere, but from four sites in particular. These are the sites of rhetorical subjectivity, rhetorical conventionality, rhetorical transcendence, and rhetorical materiality.

In Campbell's essay, to be explored later, we'll notice four main collectors into which it seems possible to distribute all the otherwise miscellaneous features of rhetorical agency. Subjectivity, for example, might be a collector for what writers such as Gaonkar would call the ideological, and what writers such as Condit or Gunn would call the illusory (Gardner 203; Young 227). And materiality (whether referring to a preformed sort of materiality, or to a "performance" of materiality, or to some other condition of materiality) might be a collector for whatever aspects of rhetorical transaction do involve an object-like exteriority (Gardner 203).

Meanwhile, convention, or conventionality, might be a collector for significations, discourses, social norms, mores, shared values or anything else functioning as a "resource" (Gardner 203) to facilitate "negotiation" (Young 228). Finally, transcendence might be a collector for "human potential" (Gardner 203), understood in terms of "choice," "questioning," "evaluation," and "responsibility" (Young 228). If so, these latter references, to human potential and the rest, would then be allusions to the role that rhetoric can arguably play in creating a better shared world for all the participants.

But to complicate rhetorical agency by folding it into four is not to suggest that any particular feature, dimension, and/or property of rhetorical agency — such as "power" — would belong, without question, inside this, that, the other, or the next of the four collectors (Gardner 203). To the contrary, it might very well remain nomadic, capable of migrating among the sites of subjectivity, conventionality, materiality, and transcendence. The point, however, is that to fold rhetorical agency into four would be to highlight the potential for an interactive, rather than internecine, collaboration among its constituents. In other words, while it's merely self-defeating to decide that rhetorical agency can be the stapling of "ideology" to "choice," it's at least workable to shift to a view of rhetorical agency as roomy enough for both subjectivity and transcendence — so long as it's understood that these, in remaining distinct and separable, would remain other to one another. Under such circumstances, rhetorical agency might prove internally heterogeneous and yet parliamentary, as in Kenneth Burke's usage, where all the participatory "sub-certainties," none of them "precisely right" or "precisely wrong," are equally "contributory" (512–13).

For now, though, we are left with a rhetorical agency so uniformly fluid, so universally promiscuous, so unanimously perverse as to constitute not a conversation but a collective misapprehension. It's a misprision such that the theorists of a voluntaristic rhetorical agency and the theorists of a deterministic rhetorical agency are always talking past one another, and always in a slaloming "monologue" that, leaving all the "sub-certainties" precisely wrong, effectively reproduces "everything in its image" (Burke 512). Thus some hypothetical eavesdropper, curious to know whether rhetorical transaction can conduce to genuine social change, would nowadays hear (out of the left side of her headset) that it can't, and also (out of the right side) that it can, and she would be left nonplussed as to how rhetoricity could ever live up to its rationale, its task of helping make things otherwise than they are.

But even if we do have to concede that rhetorical agency is both deterministic and voluntaristic, we ought to treat the concession itself, with the internal heterogeneity it actually bespeaks, as warrant for the claim that rhetorical agency is irreducible to any unitary substance, no matter how protean and promiscuous. After all, the risk we face (namely, that those aspects of rhetorical agency which we'd prefer to align with choice, free will, and the like, might yet be explained away as epiphenomenal to some overarching social logic) is not to be overcome by just any approach yielding a more complicated account of rhetorical agency. It can only be overcome by an approach which clearly divulges its philosophical commitments. Although these would probably not be commitments to an unabashed determinism (the latter obliterating any prospect of human agency), they might still be commitments to some conflicted truce between voluntarism and its counterpart.

Unfortunately, writers on rhetorical functionality are not, in fact, tending to disclose their philosophical commitments. Instead, they are avoiding the subject altogether. That's what it means for them continually to elaborate on rhetoric's means or mechanisms, while continually pleading ignorance as to rhetoric's ends or purposes — even at a time when the "fundamental properties" of rhetorical agency (questioning, negotiation, choice, evaluation) appear, in theory, to be dissolving into determinism by another name (Young 228).

To illustrate, we'll consider a couple of projects aiming to highlight rhetoric's temporality (very much as requested by Trapani in 2009), yet managing to chug along without betraying the least hint as to whether we should read this rhetorical fluidity as confirming either that (a) people can often exceed the confines of social structure, or else that (b) people are perpetually shuffled between social-theoretical concentration camps.

In "Un/Framing Models of Public Distribution" (2005), Jenny Edbauer does help us see that the so-called "elements" of the rhetorical situation, with "exigence" as a case in point, are neither particularly discrete nor impossibly indeterminate. Better to say that all aspects of rhetoric "bleed" beyond their heuristically constructed borders (Edbauer 9). So rhetorical utterance betokens an ecology, a "viral economy," where communication occurs not as instrumentalist transmission but as affective spreading — indeed, as "shared contagion" (Edbauer 13, 18). On the minus side, though, the author manages to avoid taking any stand as to whether rhetoric's contagiousness means that interlocutors remain free to exercise an inalienable capacity for choice, or whether it instead means that they are forced, through communicative processes, into just those "affective channels" prescribed for them (21). In short, we still cannot tell, not even after the author's so successfully complicating the means of communication, what it would actually be (choice? interpellation? having being born that way?) that finally animates rhetorical transaction.

It's the same story, and not by coincidence, with *The Available Means of Persuasion: Mapping a Theory and Pedagogy of Multimodal Public Rhetoric* (2012). There, Sheridan, Ridolfo, and Michel declare that they "find it essential to preserve some understanding of rhetorical agency," before adding, as if for the sake of balance, that "we do not increase our agency by pretending that it exists apart from a complex network of human and nonhuman agents" (107). Unfortunately, the authors gradually translate the term "agency" into the term "velocity" — and that's to beg the question. For, even if "velocity" does describe the career of agency, we're still in the dark as to what would go, as it were, into the agency whose career is being described. While they do offer valuable insights into rhetoric's multimodal turn, these writers neglect to divulge any fundamental philosophical commitment either way, whether to a view of rhetorical agency as bespeaking (even to the teeniest, tiniest extent) an absolutely irreducible human capacity, or else to a view of rhetorical agency as betokening a totalistic social force that's puppeteering everybody from behind the scenes.

So there's a deficiency in such works, each of them toiling (head-down) in its own vineyard, but each in its own way pleading ignorance, rather than taking any stand on rhetorical voluntarism, or on rhetorical determinism, or on both. These treatments don't, of course, tell us what to think; they tell us only what to think about. Nevertheless, in their single-minded focus on the means of communication, they siphon away attention from the ends of communication, from the question as to whatever it is that communication might be good for in the first place.

Meanwhile, there cannot, in the absence of any defensible rationale for studying rhetorical transaction, be any *justification* for researchers' gesturing to the virus-like spreading of rhetorical utterances, or for their adducing the acceleration or deceleration of such utterances within multimodal ecologies. That's because the problem with comparing utterances to viruses is the same as with comparing the contents of communication to genes (and the contexts for communication to organisms). It's that the biologistic analogy is fictive, anyway.

Let's recall that when contemporary researchers in the so-called hard sciences do hypothesize about the constitution and behavior of genes, organisms, viruses, and the rest, they're expected to ground their claims, or their speculations, not in just nothing, but, rather, in a set of assumptions as to the availability of a "code script" (Schrödinger, cited in Benítez Bribiesca 30). A hermeneutic key of this kind places boundaries on what can reasonably be said about the problem in question. An oncologist, for example, will assume that the "genetic information" necessary for understanding a particular virus must, in the first place, be "stored in a relatively stable molecule such as DNA," such that any knowledge about the molecule can, henceforth, inform any knowledge about the virus (Benítez Bribiesca 30). What's more, such an assumption will *itself* be grounded theoretically, just as the theory in turn will be grounded philosophically. Thus, in the instance of the oncologist who appeals to DNA, or to relatively stable molecules, or to code scripts, the underlying philosophical commitment might be followed all the way back to Immanuel Kant, who laid the conceptual groundwork for any subsequent confidence as to the correlation between thought, or representation, and reality.

By contrast, contemporary rhetorical scholars typically remain silent as to precisely which code script, if any, could serve as their interpretive template — and also as to precisely which philosophical commitment(s), if any, could justify their investigation to begin with. So it's no wonder when this or that study, its scope so circumspectly limited to the moment of circulation, contributes no findings to help us decide whether rhetorical agency belongs to voluntarism, or to determinism, or to both of these at the same time. The only alternative (i.e., to turning this blind eye of circumspection) would be for the theorists, the ones tasked with shaping the direction of research into rhetorical functionality, to decide whether they're committed to voluntarism, or to determinism, or to both. And, for that to happen, these same theorists would have to confront, rather than gloss over, the difference at stake among the options.

Alas, rhetorical studies presently risks vitiation by virtue of its own magnanimity, its agnosticism on the question of what could finally keep the options apart, preventing them from dissolving into one another. We find this toxic generosity at play in even the most rigorous attempts to differentiate among stances, for example, in the editorial paraphernalia for the collection *Rhetoric and Philosophy* (1990).

There, Richard Cherwitz manages a remarkable feat of translation, carefully surveying a number of rhetorical-theoretical universes in such a manner as to render them interchangeable. For, on the one side, he maintains that we should certainly inspect the philosophical assumptions that underlie the various "conceptions of rhetoric," given that those assumptions and conceptions already map out the "different ways in which the legitimacy of the rhetorical enterprise can be secured" (3, 9). But, on the other side, he maintains that any specific *choice* we might make as to "philosophical perspective," i.e., as to our rationale for pursuing Option A rather than Option B, will remain "a matter of preference" (10). So, according to Cherwitz, writing twenty-five years ago, the "significance of there being a plurality of possible groundings of the rhetorical enterprise" — groundings such as realism, relativism, critical rationalism, idealism, materialism, existentialism, deconstruction, and pragmatism — "resides in just the tensions among them," with the implication that all of the tensions are already getting along famously (xviii).

By now, it does seem that many researchers are content with just that sort of assessment. If all the philosophical assumptions do fall to our preferential disposal, then let's be charitable and uplift the lot of them in one fell swoop. Let's even prefer to suture them together, so long as we're not too individualistic about it. Since there's just the one "rhetorical world" (a continuous "landscape," a Mobius strip) for all the different approaches to address, each of the viewpoints can presumably contribute a certain something of its own (Cherwitz 4). To be sure, such permissiveness will mean that rhetoric becomes not just pluralistic, but promiscuous and protean, too. Any stretch of rhetoricity will prove as amenable, say, to existentialist analysis as to relativist analysis. But now that all the viewpoints have been globalized, we can domesticate, i.e., dismiss as merely local, any tension between the deterministic and its other.

At a moment like this, the objection might arise that it's ill-mannered to cast such aspersions upon the state of the rhetorical art. Why shouldn't everyone's theoretical perspective be a matter of preference — and why shouldn't a thousand flowers bloom, here in the one rhetorical world? Well, the answer is, in part, that "preference" isn't applicable, as we'll see when we visit Nathan Stormer's conception of the will to matter. But the rest of the answer, calling for explanation now, is that there isn't the one rhetorical world, anyway.

To accept the line of reasoning above, that which we've associated with Richard Cherwitz (but which is by now ubiquitous) would be to accept that rhetorical theory already constitutes a tableau — a self-evident body of developments for just anyone to study, and if not exactly from nowhere, then still from a standpoint that makes no difference. That's a notion of the kind which Annemarie Mol (1999) has critiqued as *perspectivalism*. It's the belief, ostensibly pluralistic, that viewpoints cannot really matter, that the "object" of our "gazes and glances" remains pristine, safely concealed from our particular ways of seeing (Mol, "Ontological Politics," 76.)

True, there's always the conundrum as to what might happen to an object that's inaccessible, that's withdrawn from us. But that's separate from the question of what might happen to an object that's disclosed to us. In the latter case, Mol would contend that any perspective we adopt must be, to some greater or lesser extent, an ontological intervention, a productive, co-constitutive interaction with that which is being observed. So, to adopt this or that viewpoint (even on something as multiple as contemporary rhetorical theory) isn't merely to adopt a stance consistent with the object. It's also to adopt an object consistent with the stance.

The claim might sound preposterous. Surely it's the other way around; surely the stance, the perspective, the viewpoint must be accountable to the object — and unilaterally so. Don't we already know as much because of those *paradigm shifts*, those unilateral sorts of development which operate everywhere, even, as Thomas Kuhn has reported, in "normal" science? For, if it's true that paradigms, or interpretive frameworks, are overthrown by reason of their inconsistency with the data, then just any scientific revolution can show that, whereas viewpoints have always been ephemeral, the objects of the viewpoints have always been fixed, waiting around for the benefit of whichever would be the next, more nearly perfect perspective.

But that isn't, after all, the best way to read a paradigm shift. It isn't that Object X prevails, surviving the shift, persisting undaunted as Paradigm A concedes to Paradigm B. Instead, as Kuhn (2000) himself explains, it's that the old object vanishes from the scene contemporaneously with its support system, and always in favor of its rival, the Object Y which Paradigm B has managed to promote instead. A quite charismatic example concerns the element formerly known as phlogiston, once a prime candidate for explaining the processes of combustion, but eventually driven out of the picture, hand in hand with its own paradigm, by the element currently known as oxygen. And if we do grant the interdependence of the object (say, phlogiston as guest) and the paradigm (say, phlogiston chemistry as host), then we're ready to concede that perspectives, too, can be ontological interventions.

Returning now to the rhetorical-theoretical object, the tableau with which we've begun, we should be able to see that, because perspectives are indeed ontological interventions, it's most improbable that the perspectives aligned with voluntarism could be engaged in building just the same reality, or world, or landscape as the perspectives aligned with determinism. The voluntaristic perspectives would be inculcating a reality where agency persisted as irreducible beyond free will. But the deterministic perspectives, by contrast, would be inculcating a reality where rhetorical agency reduced to the workings of collective force, of social logic. So the better conclusion is that rhetorical voluntarism and rhetorical determinism must belong to incommensurable ontologies, each of which entails a radically divergent set of possibilities for rhetorical transaction.

Now, with respect to normal-scientific research, Kuhn's later work shows that, while it's an error to conflate progress with unproblematic linearity, and while we "cannot get from the old to the new simply by an addition to what was already known," there is always some non-trivial change between the before and the after (15). To be sure, since any paradigm shift will involve the displacement of one *language* by another, each phase of development requires its own, carefully hermeneutic explication:

> Consider the compound sentence, "In the Ptolemaic system planets revolve about the earth; in the Copernican they revolve about the sun." Strictly construed, that sentence is incoherent. The first occurrence of the term 'planet' is Ptolemaic, the second Copernican, and the two attach to nature differently. For no univocal reading of the term 'planet' is the compound sentence true. (Kuhn 15)

Yet it's not as if the normal-scientific researcher is permitted, every now and again, to start appealing to the Ptolemaic paradigm, or to Aristotelian physics, or to phlogiston chemistry. In each of these cases, which are among Kuhn's main illustrations, a formerly available cross-section of reality — let's call it a reality as such — has long since gone away. And, now that the ontological checkbox for an entire assemblage (terms, referents, and all) has been de-selected, the language in question is no longer vital, no longer viable to speak.

By contrast, in contemporary rhetorical studies, voluntarism and determinism are practically coeval, equally permissible for researchers to invoke. Just ask Richard Cherwitz, with his insistence that, while there are, of course, alternative perspectives — such as relativism and existentialism — for the rhetorical scholar to adopt, all of these are still compatible. It's as if they're only alternative lenses upon the self-same world (where, or so one imagines, phlogiston and oxygen might be able collaboratively to explain combustion).

But this difficult contemporaneity means that we are confronted with a hermeneutic task of our own. Over there, in Kuhnian normal science, researchers can resort to concepts such as punctuated equilibrium to capture the logical form underlying "development." For while it's true that normal-scientific paradigms are separated by chronology, what's more important is that they are separated by difference, by the incompatibility that makes their juxtaposition worthwhile.

Over here, though, in contemporary rhetorical studies, it's all equilibrium and no punctuation, or at least seemingly so. Our own interpretive problem, therefore, includes recovering the missing separations, reclaiming the forgotten boundaries between rhetorical-theoretical perspectives. And since mere chronology is even less relevant for rhetorical studies than for normal science, the starting point is to acknowledge that different rhetorical paradigms do, after all, bespeak different ontologies. These alternative realities are so very much separated, so clearly punctuated by their radical incommensurability, that it would be quite the distortion to speak of them as belonging to one and the same world, or landscape, or rhetorical-theoretical tableau.

Now, one might assume that the rhetorical scholars of today, with their recourse to approaches like actor-network theory, object-oriented ontology, and so on, must already have begun contemplating the incommensurability among paradigms. They must already have started noticing the distinctions that would re-punctuate, re-differentiate, re-heterogenize the rhetorical-theoretical tableau. But exactly the opposite has been happening, with even the most forward-looking of projects tending to contribute yet more elisions through which to characterize the singularly unworkable world. That's apparently the case for Thomas Rickert's *Ambient Rhetoric* (2013), which, in addition to arguing that there's just the one reality for rhetoric to be grounded in, also lapses into what would seem to be a misreading, a misprision of what we've earlier, borrowing from Annemarie Mol, learned to call "perspectivalism."

To illustrate, we'll read just enough from Rickert to show that the author must have forgotten that alternative paradigms are not, in fact, reducible to alternative lenses on a single reality. They are not, in other words, dismissible as the "many gazes and glances," all directed at a state of affairs that's everywhere the same (Mol, "Ontological Politics," 76). To the contrary, they are ontological (not purely epistemological) interventions, each of them capable of unleashing its own objects, its own interferences, and its own possibilities for development. The disappointment, then, is that Rickert contends with perspectivalism by *trivializing* it:

> There is no "my" way and "your" way of seeing the world, no epistemological windows on a (stable, objective) world "out there" that in turn substantiates cultural relativisms. Rather, world is already implicated, and hence it both generates and participates in who we are. Worldviews, then, as ways of seeing an already preexistent world, are not originary but derive from this more fundamental weddedness to world. (xvi)

So, yes, it's hearteningly monogamous of Rickert to be over here, deploying his perspectival (existentialist, phenomenologist, and object-oriented) resources in just such a manner as to consolidate the one rhetorical world. At the same time, it's equally monogamous for other sorts of researchers to be over there, someplace else, deploying their own perspectival resources, consolidating a different rhetorical world to which we're fundamentally wedded, anyway.

To be sure, we might still be enamored with the prospect of arriving at an ambient rhetoric. If so, then all we really need to reject is the notion that it's desirable for there to be this singular environment for rhetoric's perambulations, this cohesive ecology with a nice big auditorium in the middle — a mead hall where the many heralds may gather to be heard, as in Michel Callon's (1986) turn of phrase, speaking in unison. Rickert (with his presumption that weddedness-to-world comes first, that situated viewpoint comes second) might not hear himself in that famous character from the short story, that curiously utopian figure who claims to be "not even from a place, just from near a place" (O'Connor 188). But rhetorical theorists do have to be from somewhere, and (to judge from those Graeco-Germanic intonations) Rickert must be from the paradigm that we'll later identify as the existential-transversal landscape of rhetorical agency. It's not, come to think of it, so bad a perspective to be from, not if you'd like to keep company with the specifically human actor. But it isn't the only environment accessible from within contemporary rhetorical scholarship — nor is it, not by a long chalk, the only auditorium where the many theoretical voices might gather as one.

Still, we should notice that, when it comes to Rickert's own stance on rhetorical functionality, the operative word is "preparatory" (269). It's to propose that, while there might not really be any ambient rhetoric just yet, we can still do our best to help bring it into being. In that case, if we're at all interested in trailing just such an ambient rhetoric, we should probably say the whole enterprise seems prematurely prospective, contingent for now upon the taxing (not even preparatory, but, as it were, pre-preparatory) work necessary to clear the way.

So how, under such circumstances, might rhetorical theory (writing an internally heterogeneous sentence about rhetorical agency) begin to establish not even a preparatory, but simply a pre-preparatory clearing for the consideration of (a) voluntarism, and (b) determinism, and (c) both of these together? The answer isn't that we should look around for a bigger-and-better code script, a template anticipatory enough for everything. Instead, it's that we should visit, and learn to take equally seriously, the four conceptual landscapes where rhetorical agency is already being manufactured, regardless that the (Kuhnian) hermeneutic key in force over here might differ radically from the one in force over there.

If we concentrate on dominant *terms* (rather than on proprietary critical constructs or arbitrary philosophical preferences) we can start to see that, of the four main rhetorical-theoretical realities we're to visit, each will involve a different orientation to the problem of voluntarism-and-determinism. The social-structural landscape, grounded in the subjective, will be clearly deterministic, whereas the material-semiotic landscape, grounded in the material-and-relational, will be confusedly so. By contrast, the existential-transversal landscape, grounded in the transcendent, will be strikingly voluntaristic, even in comparison to the rhetorical-humanistic landscape, which is grounded in the conventional. In this case, it'll be the former that knows where it stands, the latter, not so much.

But our project becomes that of traveling and documenting, of reporting on what each of the four ontologies can tell us about the inconsistent constitution of rhetoric's agency. Our discoveries might, in time, pre-prepare subsequent researchers to see that rhetoricity does involve not only the subjectivity, conventionality, and materiality that continually constitute things as they are, but also the transcendence that continually makes things otherwise. And, in that case, our hypothetical eavesdropper might begin to hear, out of both sides of her headset, that the productivity of rhetorical transaction is indeed such as to conduce to genuine social change, regardless that there's rhetorical determinism, and regardless that there's rhetorical voluntarism as well.

Since there's no time like the present for packing, we'll shift to a chapter on selecting some theoretical-and-practical equipment to keep our travailing light. In subsequent chapters, the third through the sixth (and toting our knapsack's worth of tackle), we'll journey to this, that, the other, and the next of the four landscapes of rhetorical agency. At the end, in Chapter 7, we'll reflect on the prospects, the options for conceptualizing rhetoric as somehow capable of making things otherwise than they are.

2.
A Four-Folded Rhetorical Agency

LET'S STOCK UP AT ONE THEORETICAL STOREHOUSE in particular, a statement which may yet turn out to offer the last word on the slippery and fluid topic of rhetorical agency. Admittedly, "Agency: Promiscuous and Protean," Karlyn Kohrs Campbell's now-canonical essay of 2005, runs through so many considerations as to imply countless features, or aspects, or dimensions of rhetorical agency. Yet the multiplicity resolves into just a few thematic clusters, and these, upon closer examination, turn out to involve only four central considerations.

Rhetorical agency involves a certain interiority, and this is the theme that Campbell addresses in her references to *subjectivity*, i.e., to the private, though socially-framed "condition" of the agent construed as a thinker and perceiver, and not only as a producer and/or recipient of communication (3). But rhetorical agency also involves a certain exteriority, and this must have to do with the *materiality* of the actually existing world — including, of course, the human corporeality which acquires "identities related to gender, race, class, and the like." That's not all there is to the sense in which rhetorical agency is enmeshed in a reality external to subjectivity. Someplace beyond the rhetorical agent is a system of public resources, referring, on the one side, to structures of "institutional power" and, on the other side, to structures of symbolicity, linguisticality, invention, artistry, and so on (Campbell 1). These collective assets point to the externality of *convention*. Still, not even the subjective, the material, and the conventional put together are enough to account for rhetorical agency proper. There must also be a place or moment for that slippage through which rhetoric, as abstract, symbolic action, comes to participate in concrete, historical action. The label which Campbell adopts for this slippage is *transcendence* — a term implying rhetoric's role in creating change, and emancipatory change, at that (8).

So we're discovering the notions of rhetorical subjectivity, rhetorical conventionality, rhetorical transcendence, and rhetorical materiality to be adumbrated in Karlyn Kohrs Campbell's own "Agency: Promiscuous and Protean" (2005). Yet it's not as if Campbell is the only theorist to have engaged these terms, or to have highlighted their interplay. It's just that she's the only theorist to have so noticeably gathered all four of them into the one place, at least implicitly acknowledging their mutual imbrication in the constitution of rhetorical agency. While each of the four terms might cover an array of more technical meanings, we should at least address their baseline usages. That'd be in the interest of keeping the denotations apart, of protecting them from dissolution into one another. For if we inspect the concepts at stake in "subjectivity," "conventionality," "transcendence," and "materiality," we find that these are not, in fact, synonymous, but clearly distinct.

The term "subjectivity" does gather up the conditions, properties, and qualities, the constructs and perceptions, belonging to the mind, rather than to whatever might lie beyond the mind. Certainly, there are disagreements as to the constitution of this interiority, which might today be understood either as that sovereign subjectivity held to have proliferated during modernism, starting circa 1650, or else as that subjected subjectivity held to have entered the scene with postmodernism and poststructuralism, or even as that ambiguous subjectivity (held to be socially-constrained in some ways but left free in others) posited in existentialist, phenomenological, and hermeneutic visions of the self. Still, those disagreements don't impinge upon the basic distinction between interiority and everything else.

It's conceivable that there might be nothing but mind. Yet there does remain a counter-conception, and this is to argue for the existence, in addition to mind, of something at least external enough to matter. The counter-conception invokes an outer dispensation, one whose spatiotemporal features (including those of our own resistant-and-malleable corporeality) often require us to engage them in a manner other than by merely thinking about them. The term *materiality* then refers to those conditions pertaining to the Great Outdoors (Meillassoux 7).

For, even if materiality itself were a projection from interiority, it might just as well be way over yonder in the "worldwide world" (Lee and Stenner 108, but also see Scarry 3).

At the same time, it's evident that the spatiotemporal features of the non-interior world include the other people, just as it's evident that we ourselves, regardless of how much interiority, how much subjectivity we may have to our credit, do not interact with those spatiotemporal features on an exclusively *ad hoc,* let alone arbitrary basis. To the contrary, we routinely collaborate, in a regularized rather than chaotic manner, with the disparate components of that outer dispensation. But the available means for collaboration (ranging all the way from the grammatical resources upholding our capacity for predication, to the guidelines we adopt for interchanges with others — and not only with human others) are not, in fact, synonymous with our subjectivity, nor are they synonymous with any features of the external world. Instead, they highlight the always-revisable relationships, the bridges, between the interior and its counterpart.

This latter consideration is worth elaborating, given that, with the entrance of a Nietszchean hermeneutics of suspicion (see Ricoeur, 1970, or, more wickedly, Greene, 1998), every conventionalized "truth," and about anything from communicative reference to sociality as such, seems unmasked as a collective imposture, a deception "binding for all" (Nietszche 146). Sure, as Nietzsche does emphasize, to be caught in a lie would leave a speaker vulnerable to the same risk as just anyone bypassing the "established conventions," this being the risk of embarrassment upon exposure (143). But to concede the point about transgression is not to concede that all of conventionality is imposture.

We don't view conventional medicine, or conventional mortgages, or conventional welding techniques, or conventional religion, or conventional warfare as if these belong merely to the conventional wisdom. Instead, we classify them with *practices*, which, rather than reducing to any "established" proprieties, frequently remain among the efficacious, if not necessarily optimal expedients for (as we say) getting things done. So convention, as in the conventionality of practice, remains halfway between the negotiated and the ineluctable. To the extent that it's revisable, such convention may seem arbitrary. But to the extent that it's practicable, then it can't be so arbitrary, after all. To the contrary, it's an interface between people and a world not built entirely to their specifications.

It does seem that collaboration can take place only with the aid of a shareable repertory for making connections, for mediating between interiority and exteriority. So, at least in the context of rhetorical transaction, "convention" refers neither to a unidirectional constraint that's imposed, as by an autonomous subject, upon the merely hapless world, nor, of course, to a unidirectional constraint that's imposed, as by an autonomous world, upon the merely hapless subject. Insofar as it describes the adoptable means for interaction, convention is a term for those variable but non-arbitrary *styles* of linkage between subjectivity and materiality.

Already, we can see that subjectivity, materiality, and conventionality are three entirely unassimilable considerations. If there were only subjectivity, then we wouldn't ever interact with anything other than our own minds, in which case we wouldn't be so very much preoccupied with the concept of materiality. On the other hand, if there were only materiality, then we wouldn't be preoccupied with any concepts at all. So, just as the concept of subjectivity argues that there's materiality, the concept of materiality, in turn, argues that there's subjectivity, and then neither of the concepts is optional. Meanwhile, if there's subjectivity on the one side, materiality on the other, and if the two sides have to be linked in a regularized, non-arbitrary manner, then the concept of convention isn't optional, either. Instead, "subjectivity," "materiality," and "conventionality" are equally mandatory, and this is for the reason that each of the three terms has to remain separable from its others in order to connect them.

But when it comes to the concept of "transcendence," we discover that the latter cannot be contained by or subsumed under the three, equally mandatory terms we've considered so far. The transcendent is that which *exceeds* any ordinary limits, whether of subjectivity, or of materiality, or of conventionality, or of all three put together. In a quite common usage, transcendence might refer simply to excellence — to a certain going beyond all expectations. But transcendence might also describe the shift from contradiction or opposition to dialectical resolution; or the shift from aggregation to mereology (such that parts are then related to wholes, and vice versa); or the shift from quantity to quality. So the most important consideration is that "transcendence" always signifies a radical departure, and a desirable departure at that, from whatever there already is. Therefore, that we do have this concept, this term for exceeding ordinary limitations, argues that transcendence cannot be coterminous with subjectivity, or with materiality, or with conventionality, or even with their collocation, but must instead be different from all three, as well as different from their intersection. In that case, "transcendence" is as mandatory as "subjectivity," "materiality," and "conventionality," regardless that it's other to them, too.

Of course the four terms are related. Subjectivity, materiality, and conventionality are related in the manner of co-requisites, and transcendence is related to them by exceeding their limitations. Still, all four terms are related through their difference. It's a difference marking, over here, the otherness intervening among subjectivity, materiality, and conventionality, and, over there, the alterity of change itself. For if alteration can be transformative, and not only recuperative, then change is what exceeds the constitution of everything.

Tetradic Due Diligence

At this stage, we can say (along the lines developed by Karlyn Kohrs Campbell) that rhetorical agency always involves some subjectivity, some conventionality, some materiality, and some transcendence, and we can add (along the lines developed by us) that these four terms — which now become the four constituents of rhetorical agency — are distinct, mandatory, irreducible, and folded together. In fact, we can say that these are so disparate and concomitant as to be axiomatic. But, in that case, rhetorical transaction must be bound up simultaneously with (a) the interiority of speakers and listeners, (b) the exteriority of the world they share, (c) the means of linkage available for connecting the interiority with the interiority, and (d) rhetoric's capacity to make things otherwise. We can use this axiomaticity, or simultaneity, to protect the constituents of rhetorical agency from dissolution into one another. For if rhetorical agency is the folding-together of four quite separable constituents, each conceptually different from the rest, then all four of them do have to participate in the rhetorical agency being theorized.

Even so, to say that the four co-constituents of rhetorical agency are irreducible (and distinct, and mandatory) isn't to say that they're given. For example, while rhetorical subjectivity would refer to the interiority of the rhetorical agent, it hardly seems likely that the interiority attributable to speakers and listeners at the time of, say, Aristotle, or of the mid-sixteenth century logician Peter Ramus, or of the baroque-era Sor Juana Inés de la Cruz, or of the enlightenment rhetorician Richard Whately could be identical with the interiority attributable to listeners and speakers today. What goes for rhetorical subjectivity must also go for the other three terms: neither rhetorical conventionality, nor rhetorical transcendence, nor yet rhetorical materiality can have stood still during those long stretches between the ancients, the earlier moderns, and us. Instead, each must continuously have become other than itself, while remaining itself anyway.

In short, if the four constituents of rhetorical agency do remain irreducible, then their irreducibility, so far as concerns their manifestation in rhetorical transaction, ought to be a proleptic, rather than a backward-glancing sort of irreducibility. They ought to be irreducible in the sense that they're processual, or emergent, or produced. For that reason, it does seem that a "productive" rhetoric, whether conceived as epistemic, constitutive, articulatory, or something else, must actually be producing the co-constituents of rhetorical agency as such.

So it's by way of rhetoric's productive irreducibility that we arrive at the epithet "four-folded." Certainly, this terminology (this network) borrows from Heidegger. He's the philosopher who holds that every *thing,* including any mode of communication, is entangled in four realms simultaneously, bespeaking earth, sky, mortals, and gods (see, for example, *Poetry,*

Language, Thought 175-175). In consequence, the label itself (that cyborg, that alliance) is also beholden to Graham Harman (2007), whose unpacking and reworking of the Heideggerian concept has proven so illuminating. It's further indebted to none other than Thomas Rickert (2013), who, in putting the fourfold to extensive rhetorical-theoretical use, does survey, and critique, and redeploy (see especially his Chapter 7) such understandings of that construct as are available from Heidegger, Harman, Bruno Latour, and others. So, already, it's possible to envision some implications for an articulation between (on the one side) earth, sky, mortals, and gods, and (on the other side) the rhetorical forms of subjectivity, conventionality, transcendence, and materiality, just as it's possible to envision some implications for rhetoricity as a "thing" whose work is to *stay* — in other words, to preserve, protect, promote — the fourfold.

However, those are not the implications to keep uppermost in mind, not during the present investigation into rhetorical agency. That's because, according to Heidegger himself, the fourfold can always be approached as a "simple onefold," in which case its disparate constituents might yet be read in terms of the "self-unified" (*Poetry, Language, Thought* 176). Sure, it'd be one thing to explore so simple a onefoldedness in the context of Heideggerian philosophy. But it'd be quite another to do so in the context of contemporary rhetorical studies, where theory, if the work of Ronald Walter Greene (2009) be any indication, seems already to have arrived at a onefold much more than simple enough.

At any rate, although Heidegger does devote "The Question Concerning Technology" (1954) to a critique (a warning against the modernistic perspective which would view everything as "standing-reserve," as exploitable), he also emphasizes that even "Enframing" — or, let's say, the very most tendentious style of perspective-adopting — should be understood as a mode of revealing (23 ff.). What's of interest here is the suggestion that any unconcealing along those lines would be an aesthetic: a paradigm for teaching us how reality (at least, how a *certain* reality) works, how all of it fits together, and how we ought to behave while we're in it. To be sure, it would also be ontotheological — in a nutshell, self-referentially circular — quite as Heidegger holds to be characteristic for all of western metaphysics (see Thomson's essay unpacking that indictment). But the point is that any such aesthetic would further become the establishment not only of an *environment* (disclosing the properly ontological existence of everything) but also of an *imperative* (disclosing the properly ontic response to everything). In that case, once we see that it's possible to begin with aesthetics and then move to ontology, rather than necessarily the other way around, we arrive at some choices as to which environment-and-imperative, which tendentious perspective, within which to be located.

In Heidegger's essay on technology, the options are binary: Either let everything be unforthcoming (such that it's to be excavated scientistically), or else let everything be fruitful (such that it's to be dwelt with poetically). But, instead of making for the sunnier side of the opposition, let's pursue the sense in which to adopt any tendentious perspective — scientistic, poetic, agnostic, or whatever — is to adopt both an environment and an imperative, in other words, to adopt a medium.

Now, when Marshall McLuhan (1964) says that the medium is the message, he means at the very least that the material-and-conceptual infrastructure for communication (spoken, written, digitized, grammatical, neurophysiological, and so on) supplies the initial condition of possibility for the message. So it's hardly surprising that the consensus among media ecologists today is that the medium is not only the message but also the environment (the context, the setting, the Burkean scene, the Heideggerian enframing) within which the message must grow (see Strate 128). Still, that's not to say the medium is only the environment — and obviously not, for it's also the message. It's, in short, a contribution, an intervention, for better or worse, into whatever's already there. That's why McLuhan refers to every technology, and to every mediatization, as an "outering" — an utterance (99).

So we're finding, if not an equivalence, then an exceedingly strong family resemblance between the Heideggerian account of tendentious perspective-adopting and the media-ecological account of mediation. On the one hand, the environment is the outering of an imperative, and, on the other hand, the imperative is the uttering of an environment. True, Heidegger, in the essay on technology, discusses only two imperatives, each attaching quite faithfully to its own environment. But the later McLuhan (1992), with his son Eric, attends to no fewer than four imperatives, all of them attaching, almost polytheistically so, to any built environment that there could possibly be. These are the tetradic laws, the quadruply heterogeneous commandments, which every enframing, every technologization, every mediatization keeps uttering simultaneously: Enhance (*this*)! Reverse (*that*)! Retrieve (the *next* thing)! Obsolesce (the *other*)!

By putting together these ideas from Heidegger, from McLuhan, and, not to forget, from Kuhn, we can arrive at a version of four-foldedness suitable for theorizing rhetorical agency. For, when we do come to look around at the four quarters of contemporary rhetorical studies, we'll see that each of them is a paradigm that mediates, enframes, aestheticizes rhetorical agency in its own way. Each of them constitutes (globally) its own world, its own tendentious perspective. Yet each discloses (locally) its own possibilities for reversing, for retrieving, for enhancing, and for obsolescing.

But, in that case, shouldn't we be looking for something rather more complicated than a fourfold — at the very least, for a sixteenfold — with all the attendant ratios and relations that such a grid would bring into view? Well, maybe so, but not until rhetorical agency has stopped looking so promiscuous and protean. For now, it's first things first, and all we need at present is to fold rhetorical agency into four. That's because rhetorical agency inheres in its *terms*, the most important of which are found together anyway.

Wherever we go, there will always be subjectivity, conventionality, transcendence, and materiality. It's just that they will be configured differently in the four different quarters within contemporary rhetorical studies. In each of those four assemblages, we will find this, that, the other, or the next of the terms being pulled into the center, where it becomes the planet, even as the three remaining terms are pushed to the periphery, where they become the satellites. So, in the interest of theorizing rhetorical agency anew, we'll reflect upon the four terms that structure every present-day version of rhetorical agency.

Disaggregating a Constitution

For simplicity's sake, let's agree that numerous treatments from within rhetorical studies, not only that from Karlyn Kohrs Campbell, do recognize there to be something subjective, and something conventional, and something transcendent, and something material about rhetorical agency. And, if the four terms are conceptually distinct, then they ought to be theoretically separable as well: Nietzsche does say, after all, that individual "concepts" can be "as bony and eight-cornered as a dice" (147). Unfortunately, our present discussions seem to leave us conceptualizing rhetorical agency as too fluid, gelatinous, and non-cornered for us to understand how rhetorical transaction would actually articulate with genuine social change.

What, then, ought we to expect from theoretical discussions addressing the concepts of rhetorical subjectivity, rhetorical conventionality, rhetorical transcendence, and rhetorical materiality? Why, we should expect each of the terms to be treated as contributing something which is not, in the final analysis, the same as the contribution of the others. In other words, whenever rhetorical agency is speaking, its co-constituents must be speaking, too, each of them adding its own heterogeneity to the conversation. That's how the rhetorical forms of subjectivity, conventionality, transcendence, and materiality could remain distinct, mandatory, and irreducible, each playing its own role in the four-folded constitution of rhetorical agency. It's also why we should think of their irreducibility as an ongoing *emergence* into difference, and not at all as the return of the given.

If we were to start viewing its four constituents as both irreducible and emergent, rhetorical agency would stop seeming so protean, slippery, fluid, and homogeneous. To the contrary, it would start looking four-folded, internally heterogeneous, participatory, and dynamic. Furthermore, rhetorical agency would begin traveling in more than just the one sense. While it would prove mobile in crossing all sorts of social locations (remaining accessible to agents regardless of their positioning), it would also prove mobile in continually becoming other than itself. But, then again, to see it that way, we'd first need a suitably rhetorical view of rhetorical agency, and of its four co-constituents, as simultaneously irreducible and emergent.

A Willfully Productive Rhetorical Agency

Such a perspective is available in an essay treating all of action, including rhetorical action, in terms of an ongoing *will to matter*. The essay is Nathan Stormer's "Encomium on Helen's Body" (2009), and among its most important "provocations" is that which concerns the purposive quality — the rhetoricity — of action in general (220). For, as the author observes,

> The media that connect one to another, the materiality of objects that signify, the embodiment of perception, the messages interpreted from the rest of nature (from genetic codes to animal behavior) — all...confound the issue of "what is *rhetorical* action" and beg us subtly but significantly to alter the question to "what is rhetorical *about* action?" (224)

In this passage, Stormer is referring to the tendency of everything to participate in a world (as in the proclivity of media to forge connections, the inclination of objects not only to signify but also to remain material, the predisposition of bodies to perceive, and the propensity of even the rest of nature to generate messages), and this is the very tendency that he's opting to call the "will to matter" (220). So, if rhetoric also tends to participate in a world, then rhetoric can be said to express the will to matter, too.

Yet the vector that Stormer is describing isn't limited to the will to power, to knowledge, to truth. Rather, it's broader, more promising and capacious than these, for it includes such wills among its internal differentiations. Indeed, the will to matter, which Stormer derives by reworking concepts from writers ranging from Baruch Spinoza and Friedrich Nietzsche to

Judith Butler, might also be known as the general, even universal "desire to persist" (220). And, as Stormer does explain, this is an imperative to flourish, not independently from others, or in spite of them, but with their interactive, mutually transformative aid. Thus the will to matter includes a will to "recognition," and a will to *change* as well. It's the impulse to make a difference, even an intensive or self-reflexive difference, just so long as the difference matters. So, if the tendency to make a difference is rhetorical, and if this is, furthermore, a tendency to change in the process of making a difference, then all of action, and not only rhetorical action, is, indeed, rhetorical.

Stormer's reading of all action as rhetorical (pushy but responsive) offers us a new way to think about the vaunted productivity of rhetoric itself. While rhetoric can still remain productive in that it's epistemic, constitutive, articulatory, and so on, rhetoric can now become additionally productive in that it's continually producing itself anew, continually enduring even as it adapts to changing circumstances. And if we do make the conceptual transition from the willful persistence of rhetorical action to the willful persistence of rhetorical agency, we can say that such agency is productive not only in its tendency to make things otherwise, but also in its tendency to adapt in response to the very changes it produces.

By now, we are better positioned to think of rhetorical agency as made up out of four axiomatically distinct, mandatory, and irreducible constituents. All of these constituents seem capable of furnishing us with some formerly-occluded evidence of rhetoric's productivity — of rhetoric's quadruple will to matter — since each of them (persistently) does remain itself even while (adaptively, interactively) becoming otherwise. And the four constituents of rhetorical agency can no longer be taken for granted, for they look to be under production, too. Their axiomaticity becomes a question, on the one side, of the more general will to matter, and then, on the other side, of the theoretical and practical work required to keep each of the four constituents durable enough to persist, but interactive enough to adapt.

By the same token, once we take Stormer's insight seriously, it's no longer "a matter of preference" as to which philosophical assumptions are to play which part in keeping rhetorical agency four-folded (Cherwitz 10). To the contrary, in a rhetorical-theoretical world where the will-to-matter is the will to make *subjectivity* matter, the most important philosophical assumptions in town are those which protect the axiomaticity of the subjective. The same logic applies to the other three rhetorical-theoretical worlds. There, the will-to-matter becomes, respectively, the will to make conventionality matter, or else the will to make transcendence matter, or else the will to make materiality matter.

So, while the broader challenge is for us to conceptualize the mechanisms through which rhetorical transaction might conduce to social change, there's also a more immediate task. It's not merely to reframe the co-constituents of rhetorical agency as both persistent (or irreducible) and mutable (or emergent), but, beyond that, to explain how they are produced with the aid of rhetorical agents as such. On the theoretical side, therefore, we'll adopt an investigative method undergirded by a philosophical commitment. It'll be a commitment, in this case, to explaining the ongoing production of an irreducibly four-folded rhetorical agency. And then, on the practical side, we'll look for evidence showing that rhetorical agents can participate in the production, too.

Our method will be consistent with the *assemblage theory* utilized in a number of social-scientific and other fields (Wise, 2005; Phillips, 2006; Marcus and Saka, 2006; DeLanda, 2006; Venn, 2006, Srnicek, 2007; Livesey, 2010). Thus the investigative framework for the project as a whole will derive primarily from the ideas of Gilles Deleuze, a thinker often invoked in contemporary rhetorical studies (see, for example, Barnett, 2005; Edbauer, 2005; Stormer, 2009; Greene, 2009; or Kephart and Rafferty, 2009).

Assemblage–Theoretical Resources

As Graham Livesey explains, the concept of assemblage derives from the English translation of *agencement*, referring, in the work of Deleuze and Guattari, not to any finished product, but rather to the very "processes of arranging, organizing, and fit-ting together" (18; see also Dosse 43). So "assemblage" (which, if rendered as *agencement*, would resonate all the more ambiently with "agency") retains a participial force, signaling that disparate elements are becoming related, forming a collectivity with emergent functionalities of its own.

However, as deserves underlining, the assembled bits and pieces are never symbolistic alone. Deleuze and Guattari do say that even "desire" is an assemblage, clarifying that assemblages don't have to be objects in a purely physicalist sense (*Kafka*, 56). Yet a Deleuzian *transcendental empiricism* posits that assemblages aren't made up exclusively of signs (or ideas), but include "sub-representative" (or "extra-propositional") experiences, these latter remaining excessive, irrecuperable (see Deleuze's *Difference and Repetition*).

It's important, therefore, that rhetorical scholars understand "assemblage" as referring to "inter-relationships" between "elements" which are emphatically "heterogeneous" (Venn 107). For were we to view rhetorical agency's four constituents as, at base, homogeneous—in the way of mere ascriptions, notions, representations—then we'd be unable to conceptualize them as separate from and irreducible to one another. They would seem to dissolve into the very significations that rendered them accessible. If so, we'd be left thinking that none of these co-constituents could actually be itself, but could only be the simulacrum of itself, and we'd remain mystified as to how rhetorical transaction could ever contribute to any social change. We should therefore view any assemblage not as a homogeneous stretch of ideation, but, instead, as a collective facility within which disparate participants, not all of them tied to human subjectivity, happen to be collaborating to produce something.

Rhetorical agency is a coalition of just that kind, its most salient functionality (though not always by design) being to produce some genuine social change. Yet rhetorical agency is a *quadruple* assemblage. It's made out of four other alliances, networks, or cyborgs, every one of them extant within a different quarter of contemporary rhetorical studies. And the four assemblages, the four "landscapes," are populated by an array of theorists, critics, and practitioners, all gathering and deploying resources for the willful production of this, that, the other, or the next of rhetorical agency's four constituents.

That's how we can account for both the persistence and adaptability of rhetorical agency, the qualities that Nathan Stormer associates with the will to matter, and with all of action. We can explain these in terms of the work that the various theorists, critics, and practitioners must be doing to ensure that each of the co-constituents of rhetorical agency does, in fact, remain persistent and adaptable. Still, in framing rhetorical agency as *assembled*, we should keep in mind that any assemblage (together with, let's add, any sub-assemblage it might be surrounding) is characterized simultaneously by "territorial sides," which "stabilize it," and by "cutting edges" of "deterritorialization," which "carry it away," such that it's able to endure even as it's able to grow (Deleuze and Guattari, *ATP*, 88). These "processes that stabilize/consolidate and destabilize/dissolve (respectively), the identity of the assemblage," do explain how the co-constituents of rhetorical agency, each associated with a different quarter within rhetorical studies, can persist while also changing (Palmås 3).

For assemblages are made up out of terms (or parts, or components) which, though they may be linked under a "dominant relation," do not reduce to such a relation (Baugh 36). Instead, the terms can migrate between assemblages, between alternative dominant relations, always retaining some of their own functionality. Indeed, with respect to any assemblage, the relations holding the terms together are "external" to the terms, these latter evading containment by any structure, configuration, or relation within which they're implicated (Colebrook 5). On the one side, a "whole" persists as an ostensible totality (as molar) for so long as its "parts" are held together in a particular relation. On the other, the constituent terms do retain their own transportable powers.

In short, even such seeming totalities as rhetorical subjectivity, rhetorical conventionality, rhetorical transcendence, and rhetorical materiality can be viewed as made up of (molecular) bits and pieces. Their components may, in principle, bring their own character along with them, migrating beyond their familiar borders, and interacting with yet other bits and pieces under an altered, perhaps unprecedented "dominant relation" (Baugh 36).

We'll therefore read each of the four constituents of rhetorical agency as belonging to a different theoretical-and-practical landscape, a terrain whose "dominant relation" is sometimes being reinforced, but sometimes becoming unsettled. We'll posit, and attempt to demonstrate, that the local theorists, critics, and practitioners are sometimes reterritorializing, but sometimes deterritorializing the rhetorical forms of subjectivity, of conventionality, of materiality, of transcendence (Baugh 36). So there's our hypothesis as to the reason for which the constituents of rhetorical agency would stay axiomatic, distinct, mandatory, and emergent. It's also our reminder that rhetorical agency might remain just as quadruple as the preceding extrapolations from Heidegger, McLuhan, and Kuhn would suggest.

Yet there is one more assemblage-theoretical precept to adduce, and it's that the assemblage, network, or cyborg (or else alliance, mesh, association: the near-synonyms abound) isn't identical with what we study. Instead, it includes our *interference* with what we study (see especially Mol, 1999). Michel Callon, for instance, has emphasized that an *agencement* is the object of the investigation as interwoven with the report on the investigation (see Palmås 2). The assemblage, drawing together some kinds of agency while giving rise to others, is therefore what emerges "in connection with" what we say about it — from our statements together with the contributions, affordances, resistances supplied by all the other constituents folded into a provisional, mutable unity (Phillips 109). Thus the act of accounting for any of these networks, cyborgs, alliances is an intervention into the very processes that bring the collectivity into being.

Triangulation

We'll need some examples to show how rhetorical transaction really could involve the ongoing persistence-and-transformation of the four co-constituents of rhetorical agency. And since we can't expect, say, "self-organization" to explain everything, we should drop to a level concrete enough to register the work performed by local actors. Let's continue drawing on Karlyn Kohrs Campbell's essay of 2005, which already attends to some particularly germane evidence, that is, in the form of a speech attributed to the African-American rhetor Sojourner Truth. For, if we gather up all of this work of Campbell's, folding it together with the explanation provided by one of Campbell's own sources, the historian Nell Irvin Painter, we discover a way to verify that rhetorical agency resides not just in the pronouncements of rhetorical theorists, but out there in the world as well.

Here, to start with, are some facts. As Painter, a scholar of African-American history, points out, it's the consensus that, in her speech of 1851, Sojourner Truth has actually—by means of speaking—"inserted black women into women's reform" and, in the process, "reclaimed physical and emotional strength for all women" ("Difference" 140–141). So, before the speech, black women are not, for all intents and purposes, really part of the women's reform movement of the mid-nineteenth century. After the speech, they are. Yet the speech of 1851 doesn't merely reflect a social change already occurring at the time. To the contrary, it helps enact, realize, or materialize the social change, creating some non-trivial infrastructure for the social change as such. The speech *itself* is an insertion of black women into women's reform, as well as a reclamation of physical and emotional strength for all women.

So, since the facts can confirm that rhetorical agency exists, the really worthwhile endeavor from now on is to explain where it comes from and how it operates. In the following chapters, therefore, we'll situate the Sojourner Truth speech of 1851 in four different theoretical-and-practical frameworks. That way, it will become caught up within such movements of reterritorialization and deterritorialization as can produce a variegated, mobile rhetorical agency.

However, we're confronted with an important methodological difficulty. For there isn't a Sojourner Truth speech of 1851. There are only alternative paraphrases, performances, productions of this conjectural artifact, some less substantive than others. Nevertheless, if we're to understand how our exemplary rhetorical practitioner could, in 1851, have inserted black women into women's reform, we'll obviously need access to her speech.

Our solution to the methodological difficulty is to undertake some *triangulation*, as by looking to the intersection where the most substantive traces of the speech agree. It's to juxtapose alternative accounts of what Sojourner Truth must have said (attending to their correspondences, side-stepping their divergences), thereby arriving at an equivalent for the otherwise hypothetical speech. In short, we'll be constructing an evidentiary text much like a bibliographical or literary recension, since that does seem a good way for us to document, i.e., from a rhetorical perspective, the concrete activity of a practitioner whose work would clarify the nature of rhetorical agency itself.

What we're given to think of as the Sojourner Truth speech is actually the choice we make when we privilege one out of two renditions. The better known rendition, and to this very day, is "a fiction created some twelve years after the event" by "an ambitious white woman," Frances Dana Gage, a journalist-activist who had served as president for the women's rights convention where Sojourner Truth spoke (Campbell 9, 13). Campbell relies extensively on the version from Gage to support her own propositions about the perverse and protean nature of rhetorical agency. Her rationale for nurturing this simulation (so replete with fabricated details as to add up to a "characterization...not supported by other accounts") is that it's "longer and more frequently cited" than its counterpart (12, 17).

Now, it's not as if we ought to defenestrate the Frances Dana Gage version of the speech, the version which Campbell is turning into a case study of rhetorical agency as such. To the contrary, it's that, since the Gage rendition is already there, what with its being so frequently cited and so on, we ought to be triangulating as much of it as we can. Indeed, so far as concerns the central claims which Gage reports, and which Campbell repeats for our benefit, it's at least conceivable that Sojourner Truth could have made them all.

So, yes, let's concede that the Gage version is the one in which Sojourner Truth's persona is the more memorably "dramatized," such that it does at least help us grasp that image of herself which the historical speaker is known to have deployed during her public appearances of the mid-nineteenth century (Painter, "Difference," 151, 154). But if so very many of the details as reported (including, evidently, most of the fireworks) are Gage's fabrications, then we should not be allowing her rendition to serve as our sole source on the speaker's rhetorical agency, or — by extension — on everybody else's. For we wouldn't want rhetorical agency itself to be a fiction promulgated by a certain mid-nineteenth century journalist, no matter how much of an activist the latter must have been.

Fortunately, another eyewitness, Marius Robinson, did publish (just a month after the event, and not, as in the case of Frances Dana Gage, twelve years later) a version of the speech that's almost as lengthy, just as interesting, and, according to the experts on Sojourner Truth, much more trustworthy than the version which Karlyn Kohrs Campbell portrays as epitomizing rhetorical agency. So, rather than settle for tracing all of Sojourner Truth's rhetorical agency to Gage's imagination, we can trace at least some of it to an evidentiary text to be built in collaboration with Marius Robinson himself.

Of course, according to the Robinson account, reprinted in Nell Irvin Painter's book, the closest analogue for the world-famous "A'n't I a woman?" (which we've inherited directly from Gage) takes the form not of a rhetorical question, but of a flat-out declaration: "I am a woman's rights." Yet it's Campbell's own use of "I am a woman's rights," the line which scholars now take to encapsulate the speech as a whole, that contextualizes our project of triangulating for rhetorical agency in the first place. For the theorist herself is the one citing that supplementary line, that flat-out declaration, as verifying that, even if Sojourner Truth never did ask whether she was a woman, she must still, in her speech of 1851, have said *something* to that effect. That's precisely as documented by this parallel statement, this "I am a woman's rights," from an eyewitness whom Campbell chooses to leave anonymous.

So we should treat Marius Robinson as an informant not only with respect to what Sojourner Truth would have said in 1851, but also to what she *wouldn't* have said. In this way, even

Marius Robinson can participate in the processes by which rhetorical agency is assembled. But, to triangulate properly, we should take some care to discount any attributions appearing only in the Gage version of the speech, and emphatically not in the version that's by far the more "reliable," the one from Marius Robinson (Painter, *Sojourner Truth*, 174; see also Lerner 59; King 137–139; Fitch and Mandziuk 18, 74). Those would be the attributions which, precisely because they belong to the fictionalized Gage rendition, we should hesitate to accept at face value, even if they do include all the makings of a quite chimerical rhetorical agent.

According to Gage (an anti-slavery feminist), but not according to Robinson (an anti-slavery clergyman), Sojourner Truth, at the woman's rights convention of 1851, speaks in a dialect most obtrusively marking her as African-American. She integrates a paradoxically and perversely authentic use of the "n-word" (Campbell 13). She notes that she's never in her life been helped into carriages or pampered in any similar respect (with the implication that, whatever she's accomplished, she's accomplished entirely on her own). She refers to her experience as a mother who has seen most of her thirteen children sold off into slavery, not to mention as a woman who, in her own person, has been forced to "bear de lash" (10). She uncovers her right arm all the way up to the shoulder, specifically in order to show her tremendous muscular power. And she directs certain witheringly pointed asides, one after another, at these hecklers, these "traditional male religious authorities" who, infiltrating and even overrunning her immediate audience, have established "a scene of great tension and hostility," right here at the 1851 women's rights convention in Akron, Ohio (9). Yet Marius Robinson (who, having once been tarred and feathered at the hands of an angry, anti-abolitionist mob, ought to remember at least the part about bearing the lash) doesn't corroborate any of these details at all (see Baker).

Yes, such details would obviously be speaking to realities faced, on the one side, by nineteenth century abolitionists and women's rights activists and, on the other side, by the historical Sojourner Truth, together with, in Campbell's turn of phrase, her "slave sisters" (14). Even so, our methodological difficulty can't be surmounted by any rehearsal of the preceding. The problem is that the very most memorable details from Gage's account — the obtrusive dialect, the close-to-thirteen children sold away, the bearing of the lash in person, the uncovering of a laborer's arm to the shoulder, even the patriarchal-and-racist hecklers are all *missing* from the Marius Robinson version of the speech, appearing only in the fictionalized version from Frances Dana Gage. So those must be the features that add up to the "characterization...not supported by other accounts" (Campbell 12). And this remains the case even if Karlyn Kohrs Campbell is bent on treating those same memorable details as if they can help us theorize the way in which rhetorical agency would actually work.

Yet we are not left with the fabricated Gage version alone, for we also have at our disposal the considerably more reliable version from Marius Robinson. Let's proceed by reflecting on the overlap between the two accounts, including the manner in which each of them helps disclose the very thesis of the hypothetical speech. In Gage, as we know, it's "A'n't I a woman?" and, in Robinson, it's "I am a woman's rights." Now, the "I am a woman's rights" (from Robinson) does seem functionally interchangeable with the "A'n't I a woman?" (from Gage). This means that we can with some justification look to "I am a woman's rights" as an alternative formulation of "A'n't I a woman?" (in other words, of whatever it was that Sojourner Truth must have been claiming). We can then ask which particular features, dimensions, or realities of rhetorical agency the various parts of this flat-out declaration might be engaging.

After all, Gage and Robinson — both of them eyewitnesses, evidentiary sources — do agree in some noteworthy ways. Among the points of agreement is that the Sojourner Truth speech is about gender, a theme clearly accessible through both "A'n't I a woman?" and "I am a woman's rights." In addition, the reality of race functions inarguably as a condition of possibility for the statement as a whole. The speech also addresses "work, mind, and biblical precept" (three central "aspects" of nineteenth-century "women's identity"), in this way refuting "all of the major arguments (biological, theological, and sociological)" then available "against woman's rights" (Painter, *Sojourner Truth*, 126; Campbell 12).

What's more, in connection with the argument as to "mind" (belonging to a nineteenth century debate over whether women and African-Americans were intelligent enough to deserve full membership in the social), there's also a kind of second-order agreement. For Robinson and Gage do, together, corroborate the role in the speech of a curious analogy, this latter again concerning the intellect of the marginalized. It's the celebrated analogy of the pint and the quart, which must therefore be playing an important part in the communicative transaction.

Finally, there's something else, separate from anything stipulated in the catalog above. Its presence is palpable in both the Gage and Robinson versions (that is, in both "A'n't I a woman?" and "I am a woman's rights"), each of which refers, though each in a different way, to the corporeality, indeed, the sheer physicality at stake in the delivery of this famous if hypothetical speech. Let's provisionally refer to the unknown quantity as *embodiment*, employing that term as a placeholder for one or another conception of materiality.

These several elements go together in a thematic bundle, and the "I am a woman's rights" from Robinson clearly serves as a more useful guide to the contents than does the "A'n't I a woman?" from Gage. It's a bundle, a package establishing rather precisely (Mikhail Bakhtin might say, "chronotopically") which utterances, which details really do have to be included in Sojourner Truth's hypothetical speech. Although we can describe the package as the core of the speech, there is a sense in which it's a lamellation as well. For the speech is assembled out of layers — of "race," "gender," "work," "mind," "biblical precept," the pint-and-quart analogy, and something quite like "embodiment." All of these lamellae must lie at the core of Sojourner Truth's rhetorical agency, since they do lie at the core of her speech. And, as we've seen, they're also articulated with "I am a woman's rights," which is the capsulation, the thesis, the handle for the speech itself. So we'll posit that "I am a woman's rights" (which, again, expresses Sojourner Truth's message at least as concretely as does "A'n't I a woman?") collocates all the points of departure required for investigating the constitution of rhetorical agency as such.

By now, we have at our disposal not only an assemblage-theoretical approach, but also some evidentiary materials to which to apply the approach. So what we should do next is firm up the agenda. We'll wish to undertake a systematic investigation of the Sojourner Truth speech in keeping with the activities of reterritorialization and deterritorialization that are taking place within the four landscapes of rhetorical agency.

An Investigative Itinerary

Let's agree, for heuristic purposes, that the "I" of "I am a woman's rights" must refer to the rhetorical agent in its aspect as the subject. Still, if the remaining string of terms — "am a woman's rights" — were there in the manner of a glorified appositive, and all in the interest of self-expression, then nothing much could happen as a result of the speech. For this would be an utterance from someone who, in 1851, is attending a convention the very purpose of which is to *generate* the women's rights that don't, at this moment, exist.

In that case, noting that the speaker's subjectivity, identity, essence, or status can't, not automatically, help her insert black women into women's reform, let's try to put that fact to use within the methodology for the study. Let's structure the investigation in such a manner as to take seriously each of the four terms in "I am a woman's rights," discovering what they can contribute to Sojourner Truth's rhetorical agency. (Or, to put it another way, let's frame each of them as an agent, an informant, speaking on behalf of one or another assemblage of its own.)

Treating the "I" as pointing to the social-structural landscape of agency, we'll accompany Sojourner Truth to a place where an axiomatic rhetorical subjectivity will look to be coextensive with rhetorical agency itself. Unfortunately, and in direct consequence, we'll soon find that just about everything she highlights in her speech will, under rhetoric's constitutive turn, seem to disappear into a sort of social-and-linguistic loop.

But we will still have to address an "am," a "woman's," and a "rights," and, as suggested above, these are not to be written off as elaborating the condition, no matter how "unavoidable," of an "I" who is only a subject (Campbell 3). So we'll treat the "rights" as pointing to the axiomatic role in agency of the conventional, and therefore as directing our steps to the rhetorical-humanistic landscape. We'll then become better placed to account for rhetorical transaction as conducing to genuine social change, for rhetoric will come into view as a mechanism for leveraging shared values in the interest of making things otherwise than they are.

Yet we'll be left wondering why someone's agency should be so dependent on a conventionality which, in privileging the shared values holding the group together, would tend continually to override, even to efface, the alterity of the group members themselves. And we'll have to consider that rhetorical conventionality, even in the form of shared values, would still need supplementation by something else, something as irreducible to rhetorical conventionality as to rhetorical subjectivity.

So we'll treat the "am" of the statement not as registering some sort of consensus, but rather as registering the diachronic and emergent character of human existence, i.e., as invoking the axiomatic role of rhetorical transcendence. The "am" will thus lead us all the way into the existential-transversal landscape of agency, where it's an authentic claim to *life*, quite untrammeled by any shared values, that counts for everything. And then we'll see that our exemplary practitioner, in deploying the life-affirming resources folded into her speech, is acting to operationalize rhetorical transcendence, as by producing some genuine social change.

Yet, as we'll notice, the existential-transversal landscape will, ironically enough, be populated by many local residents who themselves keep overlooking the full force of anybody's "am." These will be those theorists who, in tacitly assuming that rhetoric is purely epistemic, cannot help but view transcendence as ordinarily immanent to consciousness. So they will remain bedeviled by the difficulty of conceptualizing transcendence as separate from a socially-determined subjectivity. For that reason, we will have to go so far as (gratuitously) to participate in some assemblage-theoretical intervention, guiding certain of the local agents to additional resources available within their own landscape of agency. With the aid of yet another local theorist, the material phenomenologist Michel Henry, we will undertake to show that the inhabitants of the existential-transversal landscape needn't locate transcendence within human interiority, but, to the contrary, can locate it within human exteriority instead.

Even so, we will be left with another of these nagging questions, this time, as to the improbability of thinking that rhetorical transcendence (in animating genuine social change) could really involve so little as some authentically human subjectivity, some authentically human conventionality, and some authentically human corporeality, all of these sutured to an authentically human claim to exist. For an answer, we'll move on to treat the "woman's" as pointing to the axiomatic role in agency of the *material*, and, for that reason, as pointing to the material-semiotic landscape of agency. There, it will turn out that nothing is merely authentic. Instead, whatever exists — whatever seems "given" — will prove to be produced, and always from somewhere in the midst of things.

But material-semiotic production will not be symbolistic production alone, regardless that so many rhetorical theorists might prefer to treat it that way. So, when we do reach the material-semiotic paradigm, we'll have to undertake yet another intervention. We'll attempt to show how Sojourner Truth, our exemplary rhetorical practitioner, is enabled — with the aid of her radically heterogeneous allies — to produce a new reality, not out of nothing, but as the material-and-relational output of a quite unprecedented assemblage.

This latter will remain compatible with the most important themes bundled into Sojourner Truth's speech of 1851. For we'll see that "race," "gender," and "biblical precept" are *strata* (social territories) whose bits and pieces our exemplary practitioner is gathering and connecting as she speaks. The speaker and her auditors will then start collaborating, constructing an alliance with unwonted functionalities, these latter conducive to genuine social change. Thus even the exemplary rhetorical agent will participate in building a meshwork, a cyborg capable of enacting, or realizing, or materializing rhetorical transcendence itself.

3.
Subjectivity in the Social-Structural Landscape

What would happen to an exemplary rhetorical artifact were it situated within a theoretical context that defines every mode of perception, affect, thought, and ideation as socially constructed to begin with? For some insight, we'll read the famous Sojourner Truth speech of 1851 from the social-structural perspective, though we'll also turn our assemblage-theoretical attention to the manner in which rhetorical subjectivity itself is being produced, here in a landscape (an enframing, an environmentalized imperative) where rhetoric's general will to matter is localized as the will to make *interiority* matter. But, in addition to inquiring into the processes through which rhetorical subjectivity is produced, we will also ask whether the output could help even an exemplary rhetorical agent to effect any genuine social change.

Co-Constructing Constraint

With respect to the ideational formation of the social-structural landscape, we should reflect on the overview provided by Karlyn Kohrs Campbell (2005). As both a participant in and a representative on behalf of this social-structural frame, she's conceptualizing rhetorical agency from inside a "linguistic" turn nestled into a "social" turn (Crowley, "Response," 1; Lunsford, Wilson, and Eberly xxi). In other words, she's among those contemporary writers on rhetoric who are left struggling with the problem of "how to theorize the existence of an agent within the constitutive rhetorics of omnipresent ideologies" (Barnett 13).

The "constitutive rhetorics" part of Scot Barnett's formulation evokes the *linguisticality*, and the "omnipresent ideologies" part the *structured* sociality of the theoretical perspective at issue. We might notice, for example, that in the social-structural landscape of rhetorical agency, "interpellations" don't merely invite us, on occasion, to assume this or that subject position; instead, as Judith Butler asserts in "Performativity's Social Magic," they constitute the foundation of all foundationalisms, manufacturing "effects" which are "neither linguistic nor social, but indistinguishably — and forcefully — both" (126). And then the very most salient of these social-and-linguistic effects must be the production of no less than our subjectivity.

Now, one should concede that this model, according to which rhetorical agency reduces to a *subjected* interiority, has elicited some spirited critique. Nevertheless any critique would (by social-structural definition) miss the point, which is that critiques themselves can emanate only from suspect subjectivities. The more pragmatic option for us, then, is simply to investigate the concrete functionality of the social-structural perspective, in this way uncovering the attendant implications for the study of rhetorical transaction. After all, so long as subjectivity can be said to play a part in the constitution of rhetorical agency, and so long as there's an entire assemblage devoted to translating rhetoric's (general) will to matter into a (specific) will to make subjectivity matter, the social-structural model is destined to remain invulnerable, deflecting every external assault as wishful thinking.

Even so, let's at least acknowledge the influential response of Herndl and Licona (2007), who have suggested that the subject-agent might be able, kairotically, to exploit certain moments of slippage in collective structure — certain gaps at the intersections among social positions. Yet that's no refutation. It's only to affirm that, while nobody can say whether the ginormous egg precedes the itty-bitty chicken, there's still no reason not to celebrate the latter's ability to peck.

Then again, there have also been some attempts to turn the tables, to redirect the social-structural argument in just such a manner as to confound its proponents. The attempts most worth mentioning are from Marilyn Cooper (2011) and from Thomas Rickert (2013), though neither is capable of so much as impinging upon the social-structural sphere of influence, other than, perhaps, by way of theoretical fiat.

Cooper's position, as in the preamble to her "neurophenomenological" account of agency, is that, because social-and-linguistic arguments about subjectivity do tend to leave us in despair, we should start ignoring them. Certainly, any

> theory of agency that depends upon a notion of the subject is...hamstrung at the start, struggling with how to account for any action that is not either determined by or resistant to semiotic, social, political, and material others or orders. (423)

And that, as Cooper emphasizes, is why every theory conflating agency with subjectivity remains inherently defeatist, incapable of helping us see why rhetorical transaction should ever make any non-trivial difference. It's why Carolyn Miller has to explain agency as a merely subjectivist "attribution made *by another agent*," and it's "why Herndl and Licona can offer only an agent function" (i.e., a socially-determined role for a socially-determined subject), and it's why Thomas Rickert, at least in 2007, cannot envision any but "fleeting and provisional" means for "achieving resistance through subjective transformations," and, finally, it's why "Judith Butler's performative notion of agency as repetition with a difference is in the end so unsatisfying," considering that "the subject's actions are inevitably structured by the very norms that it attempts to resist" (423–424).

Cooper really is onto something: all of these social-structural, or social-and-linguistic theorizations are to *guarantee* that the agent-as-subject remain a hapless creature of the collectivity. Yet Cooper errs in maintaining that "a workable theory of agency requires the death not only of the modernist subject but of the whole notion of the subject" — even in its "poststructural, postmodern, and posthumanist" variations (423). She's mistaken precisely because there's nothing workable about wishing the subject away, certainly not so long as the entire social-structural assemblage keeps producing a socially-determined subjectivity that's, in turn, bent on continuing to matter.

As for Rickert (2013), who must have taken Cooper's criticism to heart, his position has become that deterministic theories, such as those about the social construction of subjectivity, are only world views, and that mere vagaries of opinion cannot, in the long run, make any difference, and that even the most socially-constituted of subjectivities are dwarfed by everybody's "fundamental weddedness to world" (xvi). But, again, it's Rickert who's missing the point. The inhabitants of the social-structural landscape of rhetorical agency (this factory for generating rhetorical subjectivity) have already placed the subject under the thumb of the social, and, by now, there's just no contradicting them.

That's why it's still worth our while to scrutinize the work continually taking place in the social-structural landscape. For some data, we'll return to that theoretical statement from Karlyn Kohrs Campbell (2005), to that essay which has so influentially demonstrated rhetorical agency to be coextensive with a certain collectively-determined interiority.

In surveying the relevant (not only, as it were, the "constitutive," but also the "critical-constitutive") literature, Campbell discovers that rhetorical agency in principle reduces to exactly the subjectivity proper to a creature of the status quo. Thus she prefaces her entire discussion with a somewhat disconcerting manifesto, assembled on the basis of works from Michelle Baliff, Judith Butler, Louis Althusser, and Pierre Bourdieu. It's to frame rhetorical agency as coextensive with the interiority of what we'll call, repurposing a usage from Anton and Peterson (2003), the *structural subject*.

For, while theorists such as Campbell do proceed from within rhetoric's constitutive turn, they don't consider discourse to be constitutive from scratch. To the contrary, on their account, it's actually "the community" which establishes all the "externals" governing rhetorical transaction in the first place (Campbell 9). For example, it's the group that "confers identities related to gender, race, class, and the like on its members and by so doing determines not only what is considered to be 'true,' but also who can speak and with what force." And, yes, Campbell's labor on behalf of the (incontrovertible) social-structural perspective is indeed supported by, and, in turn, supportive of, quite the rhetorical-theoretical crowd.

From Michelle Baliff, Campbell hears that the speech act

> is the sacrificial ritual which maintains the *polis* and secures the community...[B]y being subjected to gender, the self is sacrificed upon the altar of the *polis*, offered in the name of solidarity, order, harmony, peace...In this way, the political subject and the speaking subject...gain identity — recognition by the *polis* as legitimate." (3)

So, on the social-structural account, the rhetorical agent is the authorized (if thoroughly subjected) agent, dispensing occluded social forces with her every word. Besides, she's not just a political subject, but a speaking subject as well, and then her speech, if it's to be so much as registered, must be consistent with the discourse, signification, or rhetoric already approved for circulation within the collectivity.

From Judith Butler, Campbell learns that agency itself must be co-extensive with (pre-structured) subjectivity:

> "[T]he agency of the subject appears to be an effect of its subordination" or, referring to...Althusser's doctrine of interpellation, "existence as a subject can be purchased only through guilty embrace of the law." (3)

What's more, "agency is always and only a political prerogative," for "if the subject is constituted by power, that power does not cease at the moment the subject is constituted"; to the contrary, the "subject is never fully constituted, but is subjected and produced time and time again" (Butler, qtd. in Campbell 15). In that case, the perspective which Campbell is helping to construct must be one in which subjectivity is not so much "produced" as re-produced. For example, while the interiority of the rhetorical agent is said to reflect the latter's ongoing subjection (time and time again), there's not the slightest suggestion that such interiority might ever be formed other than in keeping with the dictates of the immediately given dispensation.

Next, from Pierre Bourdieu, Campbell discovers that all of communicative agency is locked irremediably into place within the status quo:

> "competence" in linguistic performance...includes "the right to speech"...the right to speak "the authorized language which is also the language of authority. Competence implies the power to impose reception." (15)

Clearly, such official control over expression then becomes an insurmountable constraint upon the very rationality which subject-agents share as members of the collective.

It's from this perspective that Campbell finally calls upon none other than Aristotle to testify on behalf of the social-structural paradigm. Citing various passages from the *Poetics* and the *Nichomachean Ethics*, and tacitly linking these to ideas in the *Rhetoric*, Campbell indicates that Aristotle's conception of "art" or *techne* (which involves a "reasoned habit of mind"), and also his conception of "thought" or *dianoia* (which refers to "the faculty of saying what is possible and pertinent in given circumstances"), not to mention his conception of practical judgment or *phronesis*, must already be consistent with the work of "Foucault and Bourdieu," where subjectivity, certainly subsuming Aristotle's conceptions of art, reason, and tact, emerges as the output of one or another governing apparatus (Campbell 6-7).

Consequently, in Campbell's social-structural assemblage, all of the (let's say) constitutive mechanisms — the commonplaces and communicative techniques at work in rhetorical transaction — turn out to be much the same as those through which the Bourdieu-styled *habitus* would generate (what else but) habits of mind. Such commonplaces, techniques, and habits of mind are now byproducts of just those "recurrent practices" which, once "internalized," provide sociality not only with "powerful engines" for "affecting and constraining future behaviors" but also with the means for controlling consciousness, rationality, and rhetorical transaction itself (5-7).

And what, so far, can we surmise of the processes through which the social-structural machine fabricates a rhetorical subjectivity that could, in turn, serve as proxy for all the rest of rhetorical agency? Well, first of all, we've seen that rhetorical subjectivity is being constructed as the interiority necessary for filling out all of the structural roles (whether dominant or marginalized) that are integral to the status quo. In other words, rhetorical subjectivity turns out to be an effect of the overarching social logic which organizes the totality. Second, we've seen that rhetorical subjectivity is also being constructed as isotopic with rhetorical conventionality, for it's now the constitutive output of just those discursive practices already authorized for use within the group. Third, we've seen that rhetorical subjectivity is being constructed as coextensive with rhetorical materiality, for it's henceforth the re-production of just those "externals" — those "identities related to gender, race, class, and the like" — which the group continually "confers on its members" (Campbell 9).

We can therefore surmise that these are processes through which rhetorical subjectivity is being assembled on the model of the *state*. For it does appear that the so-called community is a nation (with the smaller locales tucked, homologously, into a more global totality), and that collectively-determined identities are social or structural roles, and that any privileges accruing to those identities are political capital, and that constitutive discourse is the law, and, finally, that the rhetorical agent is the subjugated citizen.

Of course, there might be some more or less impassioned rejoinders, such as those implied in the work of Schrag (1997), or of Latour (2007), or of Grimson (2010). But those rejoinders wouldn't sink in, not among the inhabitants of a landscape whose will to matter is actually the will to make interiority matter, and in its most socially-determined form, at that.

Clearly, Karlyn Kohrs Campbell is correct to emphasize the communal dimension of agency, which — as she explains — has featured in discussions of rhetorical functionality since the time of the ancient Greeks. And, yes, interiorities, identities, and social roles are shaped by collective ways of speaking, just as these latter, in turn, are processed and deployed in a manner more or less consistent with prior interiorities, identities, and social roles. So it does seem that Campbell, like so many other contemporary scholars, must have every justification in the world for treating a socially-constituted subjectivity as foundational for rhetorical transaction.

After all, some rhetorical theorists have been able to show that "change" itself is indistinguishable from the *impression* of change. In "Liminal Spaces in Popular Culture: Social Change through Rhetorical Agency" (2005), Roxanne Kirkwood affirms that rhetorical agency accrues to identity, and that, even if "identity is merely a form of interpretation," it's still "real if it means something to the person claiming it" (32). As a result, since it's this sort of personalized interpretation that presumably accounts for everything, rhetorical subjectivity, all by itself, becomes the explanation for social change. Similarly, Foss, Waters, and Armada (2007) maintain that rhetorical agency is a function of the agent's "interpretation" (a "source of power" in its own right), for which reason agents always "have choices about how to perceive their conditions and their agency" (219, 223). Meanwhile, as Christine J. Gardner (2011) reports, theorists such as Joshua Gunn and Michelle Condit have entered into a debate not over whether rhetorical agency is a fantasy, but, rather, over whether it's *good* that rhetorical agency is a fantasy. Thus, after Condit proclaims that agency is a "necessary illusion," Carolyn Miller (2007) agrees with Condit, adding that agency is illusory in two senses at once (Miller 151-152). It's illusory in that it is a "constructed (or pre-constructed)" *attribution,* and in that it is "an ideological construct."

In all these cases, and many more besides, the inhabitants of the social-structural landscape have so successfully reduced rhetorical agency to rhetorical subjectivity, and have so successfully placed the latter under the thumb of the social, that it's simply irrelevant for writers like Herndl and Licona, or Cooper, or Rickert to come along and complain that the paradigm itself happens to be demoralizing.

For present purposes, though, what's important to note is that Karlyn Kohrs Campbell is not manufacturing rhetorical subjectivity by herself, nor is she lacking for allies to help her frame this subjugated interiority as governing all of rhetorical agency. As we know, "the term agency" has commonly been theorized in keeping with a "long list of terms," including "selfhood, motivation, will, purposiveness, intentionality, choice, initiative, freedom, and creativity" (Emirbayer and Mische 962). All such terms, filtered through just the right concepts from Althusser, from Bourdieu, from Butler, can readily be viewed as outputs of an ineluctable social logic. And that's how rhetorical subjectivity can emerge as quite perfectly coterminous with rhetorical agency itself (Campbell 9).

Can the Speaker Speak?

Drawing on all sorts of resources available in this first theoretical-and-practical landscape, Campbell infers that the "condition" of the agent, i.e., as a mere byproduct of social force, is by definition "unavoidable" (3). Then, to verify that rhetorical agency is the same as subjugation, she presents a dramatic illustration, a striking case, to exemplify the subjection of rhetorical agents categorically.

For, when introducing the nineteenth-century activist Sojourner Truth as the very embodiment of the rhetorical agent, Campbell emphasizes the odds *against* any such subject's ever managing to speak. Perhaps, of course, Campbell means to deliver a bit of a pep talk: where there's a will, there's a way! Even so, in rehearsing Frances Dana Gage's characterization of Sojourner Truth as "an old, illiterate, former slave woman," Campbell affirms that, when such a person is "able to speak at all" (i.e., not only to her contemporaries but also, *a longue*, to us), then that, here in quite an intriguing turn of phrase, is nothing short of "a miracle" (8-9). It's as if Campbell, in consultation with her social-structural cohorts, has happened upon an irrefragable answer to Gayatri Chakravorty Spivak's question. Yes, everybody knows the subaltern can speak, regardless that, on all the non-trivial accounts, it's impossible for her to do so.

Again, the theoretical frame which Campbell has assembled (with, again, the aid of her allies) is a perspective according to which any speaker, any nominal rhetorical agent, must be totally subjected to the state. So of course it's mystifying whenever the subaltern manages to speak anyway. At the same time, though, we should notice that Campbell, as a social-structural commentator on rhetorical agency, is committed to shoring up the theory of the theorist by undermining the practice of the practitioner. For she's demonstrating that not even an exemplary rhetorical agent ought, in principle, to be capable of saying anything that matters.

In this case, Campbell chooses to dwell on Sojourner Truth's dialect, which would surely betray something about the subject-agent's social status. The dialect then becomes important, i.e. in this representative social-structural reckoning, because it verifies that any utterance whatever would automatically become an expression of the speaker's social identity, her structural role within the collectivity.

Let's agree, without reservation, that dialect can indeed be tied, first, to one's ascribed identity ("race, class, and the like") and then to one's subjectivity, in this way lending credence to the argument that it's never really the rhetorical agent who speaks, but always a pre-established sociality that speaks through her (Campbell 3). To be sure, it's only in a certain fictionalized version of the Sojourner Truth speech that any of the non-standard dialect exists to begin with. Nevertheless, since we ourselves are concerned with the *work* that the social-structural investigator is having to perform, namely, the work of undermining the practice of the practitioner, we should take a moment to examine Campbell's preferred uses for the (bogus) dialect which Frances Dana Gage, our theorist's privileged source in this regard, has sutured to Sojourner Truth's statement.

The difficulty is that — by Campbell's recurrent admission — the non-standard dialect isn't authentic in the first place (12–13, 18). Therefore, to derive Sojourner Truth's rhetorical agency, as Campbell does, from a spurious dialect, and to place so much emphasis on this same non-evidentiary dialect (as, on the one side, "degrading" and "deformed" and, on the other side, authentically evocative of the speaker's identity) does look to be quite the social-structural sub-routine. If it's defensible, that's not on the basis of any historical evidence, but, rather, on the basis of a theoretical perspective which reads rhetorical agency as manifesting just that interiority proper to a minion of the state.

Thus we arrive at some corroboration for the assemblage-theoretical premise that the investigator, too, is always among those who are producing the assemblage under investigation. For Campbell divulges that, once upon a time, she'd been confronted with a problem of editorial craftwork that must have been a problem of theoretical production as well. She'd had to decide whether to retain or else to excise Gage's interpolated (degrading, deformed, inauthentic) dialect:

> When the text of Gage's version of Truth's speech was published in *Man Cannot Speak For Her*, I removed the dialect that smothers the speech with racist stereotypes...I now believe that it was wrong to do so, although it could not and should not have been published as originally written without the kind of analysis done here. (14)

With respect to Campbell in that former role as editor, we should indeed recognize the challenge she faced. Yet, with respect to Campbell's present role as theorist, we cannot very well say that she's merely attending to the evidence as given, that she's simply inspecting something inherited from elsewhere. To the contrary, she is demonstrating, and before our very eyes, that she is *still* engaged in generating the materials that she's supposed to be uncovering. After all, she's drawing her data from, and basing her analysis on, a speech which sometimes includes the bogus dialect but sometimes excludes it, all depending on the theorist's own interest in making the bogus dialect matter.

What the demonstration itself demonstrates is that Sojourner Truth is not the only rhetorical agent in town — that a theorist like Karlyn Kohrs Campbell can be a rhetorical agent, too, right along with the "old, illiterate, former slave woman" whose activity she's studying (9). It's just that the theorist in this case happens to be working to advance the social-structural perspective on rhetorical agency. Under an environmentalized imperative like that, subjectivity is so thoroughly constrained, so utterly determined, that it's a miracle when anybody speaks at all, let alone when she's heard over the noise of her identity.

An Ineffectual Agency

The social-structural perspective, ostensibly "constitutive," illustrates the workings of a social-and-linguistic loop. In this view, rhetorical agency is a circuit, with some socially-enforced structure at one end, some socially-constrained subjectivity at the other, and some socially-determined signification in the middle (connecting the two ends by filling up the conceptual space between). Rhetorical agents can then be theorized as merely operationalizing the constitutive forces that create the rhetorical agents to begin with. Indeed, that must be what Campbell has in mind when she writes that "agency is constitutive of collectivities…just as collectivities are constitutive of agency, however paradoxical that may seem" (5).

Even so, in our present investigation, it's not social-structural theory in isolation, but, rather, in conjunction with a certain case study (involving Sojourner Truth's famous speech) that's to illustrate the workings of a subjected rhetorical agency. Of course, it would also be manageable for us to dispense with the case study altogether. We might settle for quoting one or another of the assertions rehearsed above — say, the complaint that, in theories like that of Judith Butler, "the subject's actions are inevitably structured by the very norms that it attempts to resist" (Cooper, "Rhetorical Agency," 424). Yet, insofar as we are acting as assemblage-theoretical researchers, our task is not, in fact, to rehearse complaints; it's to disclose connections and consequences. Thus we should simply ponder the destiny of our selected artifact, were the latter to be read in keeping with the social-structural paradigm. What would happen, more than likely, is that the speech would prove not to manifest very much rhetorical agency at all, whether for (a) the audience to whom Sojourner Truth would be speaking, or (b) the constituency she'd appear to be opposing, or (c) the listeners who hadn't yet made up their minds.

To begin with, the speech, according to social-structural logic, ought to do next to nothing for just that audience with which the speaker would seem the most closely identified. In this case, Campbell assumes that the audience in question would comprise all the disempowered African-Americans and women of the mid-nineteenth century, in other words, all the sorts of disenfranchised persons with whom Sojourner Truth could be affiliated, as if automatically so, by virtue of her race and gender. Yet our own observation should be that, were she really speaking for a constituency unified by its own discourse, our exemplary rhetorical agent would not be able to say anything that could matter. The unified community of disenfranchised African-Americans and women would already prefer that they be granted their missing rights, and then nothing Sojourner Truth might say in support of that preference could make any difference.

Certainly, as one might extrapolate from any public speaking textbook, Sojourner Truth may have in mind purposes other than to convince. She may be seeking merely to reinforce the predilections already in place. She may even be hoping to motivate some outright action. But, then again, those outcomes couldn't matter either, not in a world where socially-constituted subjectivities would already determine which socially-constituted trajectories may prevail.

On the other hand, if the speech were to be read in rigorous keeping with the social-structural paradigm, then it ought to do even less for the speaker's opponents than for her supporters. In a social-and-linguistic view such as Campbell's, speech itself ought to be the automatic reinstitution of the "unavoidable" condition of the subject (Campbell 3, 12). So, under a model where rhetorical agency attaches to membership within the status quo, somebody speaking for the minoritarian position oughtn't, in principle, be able to out-shout the majoritarians. To do that, the exemplary rhetorical agent would have to speak in so miraculous a manner as to convert her own, marginalized identity into a source of empowerment, and against the very forces precluding such empowerment in the first place. But is that really what we should expect from a theoretical perspective where the more powerful subjectivities and/or discourses would forever be keeping their weaker counterparts at bay (constituting them, again and again, as insignificant)?

So, if it's the case, as on the social-structural reckoning, that neither the position of those already constituted as the speaker's supporters, nor the position of those already constituted as her opponents could be altered by anything the speaker might say, then, by process of elimination, we should conclude that all of the claims, themes, and images bundled up into Sojourner Truth's speech must be there for the benefit of quite another set of listeners. They ought to be there for the benefit of the *undecided* auditors, those who hadn't (in connection with this particular debate) been constituted either way.

Subtracting from Rhetorical Practice

At the risk of lapsing into some instrumentalism, let's agree that the speaker must be thinking to create a coalition between her supporters and the as-yet undecided auditors, i.e., as a practicable way of swelling the pool of subjectivities in favor of extending equal rights under the law.

Therefore, from now on (in the remainder of the study, and not just while we're here in the social-structural landscape of agency), we'll assume that Sojourner Truth is speaking mainly to the undecided, the auditors in the middle, and that not only "I am a woman's rights" but also the rest of her speech (comprising *gender, race, mind,* and so on) is primarily, though not exclusively, for them.

Unfortunately, so far as would concern any undecided auditors, every term in "I am a woman's rights" would start disappearing if read from the social-structural perspective. The "I" would refer to a black person, and therefore to someone who (at a time when most of the African-Americans are enslaved, and the rest politically invisible) is practically a non-entity, hardly a figure for the undecided auditor to identify with. By the same token, the "woman's" would refer to a merely subaltern contingent, just as the "rights" would refer to a freightless counter-factual. For, in the historical setting for the speech, it's the very reality of women's rights (to say nothing of African Americans' rights) that is still the unknown quantity. And then, should the majoritarian contingent prove anywhere near as hostile as Gage reports, and as Campbell continually insinuates, so much the worse for Sojourner Truth's (tainted) identification with all the other women's rights activists, outliers as they are to begin with. Thus the various social-structural tenets already invite us to conclude that much of what goes into the speech (all of it there to develop "I am a woman's rights" as its kernel, its thesis) must be squandered on behalf of a project *lacking* in agency for the undecided auditors.

By now, in noting the likely effacement of every term in "I am a woman's rights," we have simultaneously encountered the likely effacement of at least two of the most important themes folded into the speech. The elements in question are *race* and *gender*. After all, from the perspective of the undecided auditors, the speaker's very dependence upon the two marginalized identities, one that of an African-American, the other that of a woman, must be subtracting from, rather than adding to, her rhetorical agency. But we'll continue regardless, folding some of the remaining features of the speech into the social-structural paradigm as well.

As we glean from reading Campbell between the lines, there is available, in contemporary theory, a quite reputable explanation as to how even an "old, illiterate, former slave woman" might exercise agency in the face of a racist, sexist, and generally oppressive form of sociality (Campbell 9). It's that the exemplary rhetorical agent can harness the *constitutive* power of the discourses circulating within her collectivity.

For, as Campbell indicates, the Sojourner Truth speech is situated within a set of nineteenth-century "principles" or commonplaces (14). These betoken (on the one side) the then-progressive discourses of natural rights, abolitionism, and women's rights, and (on the other side) the then-conservative discourses of traditional religious authority, of legalized and monetized racism, and of patriarchal, "elitist conceptions" of "true womanhood" (10, 14). So, according to Campbell's social-structural reasoning, what must be happening in 1851 is that the speaker is seeing to it that the progressive discourses come to exert all the more authority than do the conservative discourses. And it is marvelous indeed to think that the speaker could exercise rhetorical agency by invoking precisely those commonplaces held at bay in the operations of a backward-looking dispensation. After all, in its departure from the ideologies then hegemonic within the status quo, a minoritarian discourse of natural rights would appear replete with liabilities, not assets, for anybody deploying it.

To support her argument about the collective basis of agency, Campbell avers that "without the communities represented by abolitionism and woman's rights, the natural rights principles underlying the arguments as reported in the newspaper accounts and incorporated into Gage's versions of the speech would not have been available to Truth" (14). The point, let's recognize, is not that the speaker becomes an agent by appealing to natural rights; it's that she becomes an agent by appealing to just any previously-approved discourse, for example, that of natural rights. For, according to Campbell, it's by parroting the principles already acceptable to her target audience that our exemplary rhetorical agent refutes "all of the major arguments (biological, theological, and sociological) against woman's rights" (12).

On this view, the speaker would be invoking natural rights to argue that the rights of women and African-Americans ought certainly to be added into the set of civil, legal, or statutory rights from which they are missing. So, to discover how dubious is this (nominally "constitutive") picture, this scenario in which discourses are sources of agency simply because they're collectively authorized, let's investigate the claim that for someone to invoke a minoritarian discourse could convert her into a rhetorical agent just like that.

If we reflect that the social-structural perspective would require the discourses in question to be hierarchically disposed (i.e., within a sociality modeled on the state), we'll see that a discourse which is locally influential really ought not to be any match for a discourse which is globally normative. As a result, and on the social-structural reckoning itself, we should expect any hypothetically undecided audience to become increasingly inclined toward the status quo, rather than toward a speaker who is limited to deploying arguments which, though perhaps inspirational for her own disempowered "community," are immediately recuperable into the logic organizing the society at large.

Now, the doctrine of natural rights most obviously at issue in the Sojourner Truth archive would be that reflecting the Jeffersonian division of rights into those which are alienable and those which are not, the latter including the rights to life, liberty, and the pursuit of happiness. One wouldn't, however, have to be a constitutional scholar to know that these inalienable rights of the mid-nineteenth century do co-exist with their legalized effacement, both in the practice of slavery, and in the disenfranchisement of women.

Simply on the face of it, we have an inequality between the discourse of natural rights and the discourse of civil or legal or statutory rights. And, probably like the historical audience, we notice this to be an outright imbalance, rather than some sort of stalemate. For just anyone can look around and see that reality, circa 1851, is weighing in overwhelmingly on the side of the state, whose actions have long since verified that even natural rights are subsumed under legal or statutory rights.

Even so, according to Campbell—whom we're consulting as a representative for the social-structural perspective more generally—the speaker in the case study is further warranting her claim (for the expansion of legal rights such that they also accommodate natural rights) with the aid of examples drawn from personal experience, and scriptural precedent, and just plain common sense. All of these are said to be showing that women like Sojourner Truth do remain ontologically or "naturally" equal to men, for which reason they should be granted their missing legal rights as well. Yet these are precisely the sorts of examples that ought to be neutralized under a perspective where somebody becomes a rhetorical agent, first, by virtue of her "unavoidable" subjection under the social dispensation, and, second, by virtue of her fluency in precisely such commonplaces as those to which only a local, pre-constituted, and grievously out-flanked audience could respond (Campbell 3).

Campbell reports that the reason for which Sojourner Truth so carefully "details the heavy fieldwork she has done" is that she's thereby showing that women can be as physically strong—and hard-working—as men (Campbell 10). So, in order to establish that she, exemplifying all the rest of the disenfranchised, is certainly entitled to the legal rights that are currently missing, the speaker insists that she has long since proven herself qualified to fill out the social role of just any manual laborer. Yet it's difficult to see why this, from the perspective of an undecided audience, should be an argument constituting the disenfranchised as entitled to the full range of legal rights. It could as easily constitute them as entitled to continue performing the heavy fieldwork.

But then, as Campbell would have it, Sojourner Truth also cites some scripture to prove that, because the equality of women with men is woven into the universe, it should certainly be protected by the state as well. For this must be the point not only of the speaker's referring to "the Virgin birth, which presumably is a religious belief accepted by her opponents," but also of her referring to the "power" of Eve—a power quite undeniable even by the speaker's racist-and-patriarchal hecklers, considering that these latter would be none other than the "traditional male religious authorities" to begin with (Campbell 9, 11). Regrettably, it's still unclear that Eve and Mary would, in the middle of the nineteenth century, have had their own legal rights, in which case it's not self-evident that to invoke those figures would immediately constitute all the rest of the women as entitled to legal rights by association. On this count, too, the hypothetically undecided audience wouldn't have any compelling reason to side with the speaker, rather than with the status quo.

Finally, or so Campbell argues, Sojourner Truth clinches the deal by emphasizing her own intelligence. The idea would be that women like Sojourner Truth are certainly entitled to legal rights because of their wit, their all-around cleverness. And it is indeed in connection with the problem of *mind* that the analogy of the pint and the quart comes into play.

One hardly need argue for the importance of tropes—vivacious imagery, *enargeia*, figures of speech, comparisons of all sorts, conceptual metaphors, frames, and the rest. Such features of technique have always been associated with rhetoric's storied power, now commonly labeled "constitutive," to help interlocutors see themselves (their situations, their problems) differently than before. Yet Campbell, for all her social-and-linguistic presuppositions, runs into inordinate difficulty explaining how the pint-and-quart figure would work. Indeed, she comes close to suggesting that the analogy might, after all, have a little less to do with highlighting women's intelligence than with showing how skillfully a woman can elicit charitable donations.

But here, in any case, is how we find the analogy presented in Gage, that is, in Campbell's preferred, if often dubious, source on our exemplary rhetorical agent:

> "Den dey talks 'bout dis ting in de head; what dis dey call it?" ("Intellect," whispered some one near.) "Dat's it, honey. What's dat got to do wid womin's rights or nigger's rights? If my cup won't hold but a pint, and yourn holds a quart, wouldn't ye be mean not to let me have my little half-measure full?" (qtd. in Campbell 10)

And it's noteworthy that the following is all that Campbell can find to say about the pint and the quart as a constitutive, metaphorically-validated way of elevating the discourse of natural rights so that it may henceforth compete with, and even overcome, the discourse of legal rights:

> The implied argument against women's rights [has been] that women lack the mental capacity for political and economic rights. [The speaker] rejects the relevance of this issue to civil rights for women or African Americans. Note that her words presuppose natural rights principles, that rights are not conferred but inhere in persons. The case of equality of opportunity is made with a vivid figurative analogy — even if my cup holds less than yours, are you so mean you won't give me my little half measure? (10)

Consequently, with respect to "mind," Campbell's social-structural perspective does lead her to conclude that the speaker must be deploying the resources of language in order to frame natural rights as trumping legal rights, even if that also requires shaming the audience in the process.

Yes, but let's think about what would be happening here — at least, on an appropriately rigorous social-structural account. The metaphor of the pint and the quart, that clever analogy, would be *separating* the discourse of natural rights from the discourse of civil rights, leaving the two discourses talking past each other. Exactly as Campbell concedes, the intelligence of women and/or of black people would prove irrelevant to the question of social, legal, or civil emancipation. As a result, the hypothetically undecided audience would be left with even less reason to side with the speaker than ever before, since the speaker herself would be arguing that natural rights had nothing to do with legal rights, anyway.

Thus it turns out that, from a social-structural perspective, the metaphor of the pint and the quart couldn't be so very much "constitutive," after all. Instead of creating a new way of seeing (such that those auditors subscribing to legal rights could perhaps find themselves connected with those subscribing to natural rights), the "vivid figurative analogy" would, more than likely, invite everyone to return to the shelter of the old discourses, the old rationales for remaining undecided, to which they'd been adhering all along (Campbell 10).

Yet the question remains, especially for those who are not social-structural theorists, as to how the exemplary rhetorical agent, were she limited to recycling a weakly minoritarian discourse, could effect any social change whatever, i.e., in the face of a robustly hegemonic discourse. Again, just anybody circa 1851 might look around and see that, while metaphysical rights can't be withheld, legal rights obviously can, in which case there's no, as it were, structural reason to link the one kind of right with the other.

What Else Is Wrong with This Paradigm?

In opting for an assemblage-theoretical approach, we're having to ponder the processes through which the four different versions of rhetorical agency are being manufactured, even if one of the versions might prove only to be reinforcing the social conditions already in place. So let's consider that the social-structural perspective, where rhetorical agency becomes indistinguishable from rhetorical subjectivity, is actually a way of flouting the assemblage-theoretical approach that we ourselves have begun to implement.

As we know, assemblage theory (in the variant adopted for this investigation) holds that collectivities are built out of components — resources, agents, participants in general — that are irreducible to any of the relations in which they're implicated. So an assemblage-theoretical perspective leaves open the possibility that a term like "subjectivity," though it might, in some respects be shaped by those communal structures into which it's folded, might also, in other respects, exceed the constraints that are imposed by the structures themselves.

In the social-structural perspective, by contrast, all terms are claustrated, for they are synonymous or isotopic with a socially-determined interiority. In this case, subjectivity becomes the planet, and then conventionality, transcendence, and materiality become the satellites. Yet all of the terms exist as fully internal to their relations, as ineluctably bound by them. That's what it means to argue (as Campbell does, albeit with the help of an entire social-structural support system) for speakers as miniaturized chunks of sociality, as creatures of a collectivity that subjectifies them, determining, on the one side, what's considered to be "true," and, on the other side, "who can speak and with what force" (Campbell 3). Thus, in a landscape where rhetorical subjectivity arises within a closed, self-contained system (a social-and-linguistic loop), it necessarily remains the only conceivable source of rhetorical agency.

A Chimerical Agency for a Colossal Agent

That this is not just a theoretical but also a practical setback becomes clear when we consider that any social-structural researcher will finally have to justify all of rhetorical transaction by theoretical fiat. Let's again reflect on the plight of Karlyn Kohrs Campbell, who is obviously cognizant of the (defeatist) ramifications of the perspective she espouses. To assure subsequent researchers that rhetoric does, somehow, retain its own role, its own task, even where theory leads to the opposite inference, Campbell invites them to trust in the constitutive powers of "alchemy" (13). Regardless that Frances Dana Gage's version of the Sojourner Truth speech is in so many ways bogus, we can pretend that it isn't. Instead, we can turn to what we "imagine" to be the "originary moment," with its "play of ideas," its "metaphors," its "interaction between Truth and her opponents" (Campbell 14). That's how we can *wish* the rhetorical agent into being. After all, rhetorical agency can inhere — if only we'd like it to — in any signs whatever, even those belonging to a "fictive recreation" (13). For example, we can derive, from the famous fabrication by Francis Dana Gage, a made-up Sojourner Truth to serve "as an icon and symbol for her slave sisters." Thus we can attribute some rhetorical agency to this impossible speaker's "words as we imagine her to have spoken them," even when we have every reason to believe that the "words" belong not to Sojourner Truth, but to a simulacrum constructed, twelve years after the fact, by — as Campbell herself explains — an "ambitious white woman."

It's as if we can now have the best of both expedients, juxtaposing the basket of critical-constitutive rhetoric with the basket of just plain constitutive rhetoric, and proclaiming rhetorical agency to be hidden inside whichever of the baskets we prefer. If we'd like to privilege the critical-constitutive rhetoric, then we can affirm that the rhetorical agent must be the subjected minion of the community (i.e., the seamlessly totalitarian state, producing all the marginalized interiorities, ruling on whatever is to be considered true, stipulating exactly who may speak, and with exactly what force). But if we'd like to privilege the constitutive rhetoric proper, then we can affirm that the rhetorical agent is only on occasion a disempowered structural subject, and, at other times, a colossal individual, inherently capable of bending the social to her will, and all of it just like that. In this case, she can come into view the very minute that the marginalized subaltern spins around, turning suddenly into "a very tall, strong woman of great presence with a commanding voice in speech and song," someone with great "wit…skill at repartee…command of metaphor, and…courage in facing hostile audiences" (Campbell 9).

The problem for Campbell, though, is that to deploy all these social-structural tenets (and to invoke a simulated Sojourner Truth) requires that she undermine the mountain of concrete evidence presented by the historians whom she herself is citing, historians such as Nell Irvin Painter. All of this historical evidence is to suggest that rhetorical agents might be produced in some way other than through absolute subjugation and/or theoretical fiat. But Campbell, regardless of all that Painter in particular has done to demystify the colossally authentic speaker, wants us to preserve that canard so we can ("constitutively") exploit it.

So here's an illustration of the manner in which the social-structural perspective would (to repurpose a term from Paul Virilio), endo-colonize just any source materials it happened to fall upon: "What Painter fails to understand is that Gage's fiction has a dramatic agency as a performative text that is greater than historians' facts" (Campbell 14). Clearly, if Campbell is choosing to trivialize the argument from "facts," then that's because she's attempting to protect the argument from performativity. Trapped inside a linguistic turn, the latter embedded within a social turn, a social-structural theorist like Campbell has no access to anything more substantial than wishfulness, or desire, or theoretical fiat when it comes to explaining how rhetorical transaction could ever make any difference under the present dispensation.

In short, our main discovery (on this first leg of the trip) has been that the social-structural perspective is a machine for *debilitating* the practitioner, for weakening rather than empowering the exemplary rhetorical agent. Yet the local theorists, here exemplified by Karlyn Kohrs Campbell, keep overlooking their own role in perpetuating this framework within which communities are totalitarian states, discourses are constitutive in the manner of the law, and subjectivities are homologous with the structural relations into which they're embedded. Sadly, in their determination to construct a constrained, victimized rhetorical subjectivity, the latter coterminous with all the rest of rhetorical agency, such researchers have begun jeopardizing rhetorical transcendence as well. They are already reporting that, were any rhetorical agent ever to speak in a manner conducive to social change, it would necessarily be by miracle.

4.
Conventionality in the Rhetorical-Humanistic Landscape

BACK THERE IN THE SOCIAL-STRUCTURAL perspective on rhetorical agency, every standardized practice associated with rhetorical transaction would resemble an artifact of subjectivity, thus risking quite merciless interrogation under the light bulb of "normativity." Therefore, to understand how rhetorical conventionality might somehow tamper with, rather than merely reinforce, the present dispensation requires that we shift to a world in which this second aspect of rhetorical agency can indeed make things otherwise than they are. Having addressed the "I" of "I am a woman's rights, of that thesis-like claim which features so prominently in our case study, we'll now treat the "rights" as leading to a place where rhetorical conventionality is central, and where the local theorists are among those protecting its centrality (Campbell 3).

De-Leviathanizing the Normative

Here, in the rhetorical-humanistic landscape of agency, rhetorical transaction is animated not by nothing, but by ideals, visions of the good, and so on, all of which, because they function as "terms" irreducible to their "relations," remain separable from social structures and the like (Baugh 36; Colebrook 5). Part of our responsibility, then, is to inquire as to where such collective guidelines could be coming from. After all, from the vantage point of our own (assemblage-theoretical) approach, even shared values have to be seen as produced — maybe not created from scratch, but, in any case, continually raised to salience.

We should therefore consider the work of at least some of the actors who have been producing all of these commonly accepted measures to begin with. Although the label "rhetorical-humanistic" derives, somewhat indirectly, from the work of Michael Leff (2003), we'll treat the activity of such theorists as Bryant (1953), Wallace (1963), and Weaver (1970) as exemplifying the rhetorical-humanistic drive to shore up rhetorical conventionality precisely by assembling it on the basis of values held in common. According to these writers, rhetorical agency isn't just any stream of transparent norms, but, rather, a bridge between *embodied* subjectivity (or experience) and *collectivized* subjectivity (or shared guidelines).

Donald Bryant emphasizes rhetoric's concern, on the one side, with our "thoughts, feelings, motives, and behavior" and, on the other side, with our "ideas" and "values"—with what we as members of a collective know about and consider "worth doing" (412-13, 415).

Rhetorical agency, then, is an emergent property of, as Bryant explains, the "whole" person, in whom are hybridized the materiality of, say, behaviors, and the sociality of, say, ideas (Bryant 414). Karl Wallace, too, highlights the role of "ethical and moral values," and he affirms that rhetoricity draws not only on functions belonging to "social rewards and sanctions" (from which we learn "right" and "wrong"), but also on functions belonging to "the individual organism" (240, 244). Thus rhetorical agents are linked through "commonalities of meaning and partial identities of experience," and these, again, are the links between the materiality of an organism and the sociality of a collective (239). Similarly, Richard Weaver insists that rhetoric seeks to engage (what else but) the "whole" person—much of whose wholeness is sustained through "this subjectively born, intimate, and value-laden vehicle which we call language" (Weaver, "Language," 316). All of these writers are building rhetorical agency out of an articulation between, on the one side, the evaluative criteria shared within the community and, on the other side, the sort of embodiment that's universal among all of the group members.

To size up this notion of shared values, we'll turn to the account Weaver offers in "Language Is Sermonic"—a statement quite canonical for the rhetorical-humanistic perspective. Weaver acknowledges rhetoric's amphiboly: on the one side, it refers to an "independent order of goods," involving "a "vision of how matters should go ideally and ethically"; on the other side, it proceeds from "an order of desire," involving the "particular situation," the "special circumstances of the auditors" (309). Here, we have a distinction between the aspect of rhetoricity that goes with communal guidelines, operating ideally and ethically, and the aspect that goes with embodiment — operating specially, particularly, situationally.

Even so, the presumption is that there are commonplaces for mediating between the timeless, "independent" order of goods and the *dependent* special circumstances, for such are the commonplaces, the reconciliatory ways and means, that we're now calling shared values.

They're like ribbons, streamers, fixed at the one end (where they're nailed into the independent order of goods), but free at the other (where they can be manipulated over to just any situation, within the dependent order of desire, where they're applicable). We can therefore say that rhetorical-humanistic agency is a hybrid between the cultural-anthropological and the biological-anthropological, for it's as much anchored in some unspecified range of deeply entrenched, yet redirectable social guidelines as it is in the Standard Human Complement.

The term "Standard Human Complement" refers in this study (though it originates in certain slightly ironic usages from elsewhere) to whatever array of traits and faculties may be held to define human beings as (a) members of a single, notably embodied, fallible species, and (b) capable of thinking and communicating so as to reshape the objects, problems, and situations that they're faced with (Lodge 299; Thomas and Turner 95). Such an array, such a Latourian "black box," working well enough that almost nobody worries about its "internal complexity," could certainly collect a number of those items appearing in the "long list of terms associated with agency": "self-hood, motivation, will, purposiveness, intentionality, choice, initiative, freedom, and creativity" (Latour, *Reassembling*, 304; Emirbayer and Mische 962).

However, according to the rhetorical-humanistic model, while people do possess a general sort of agency just by virtue of being people, this inherent agency isn't, in isolation, enough to make them *rhetorical* agents. For that, there needs to be a connection between, over here, the inalienable properties of the human actor and, over there, the collective properties (most of all, the locally-shared values) characterizing the group to which both the speaker and the listener belong. With the linkage in place, then — yes — everyone is now a rhetorical agent, and also, for that matter, a cyborg. The name for this rhetorical agent (this network) is, as we've seen, the *whole person*. And what makes the actor "whole" is that she is the complete reconciliation between, on the one side, those ideational and affective guidelines characteristic for her group and, on the other side, the Standard Human Complement which everybody possesses simply by belonging to the same species.

So, while our rhetorical-humanistic competencies belong to us as members of the worldwide, anthropological community, our rhetorical-humanistic shared values belong to us as members of the local, historical community. But rhetorical agency is still not some special power, accruing to an elite. It's the ordinary ability to link values and object(ive)s within a collectivity where differences are shallow, constituting an overlay easily rubbed off to disclose the continuity beneath. After all, just anyone possessed of the Standard Human Complement can help her neighbors come to see themselves, their problems, their situations in terms of the shared values which have always kept the community together.

For language is, on this view, *constitutive* only in the sense that it's a humble "system of imputation, by which values and percepts are first framed in the mind and are then imputed to things" (Weaver, "Language," 316). The percepts, as manifestations of the Standard Human Complement, can take care of themselves. Therefore we, as investigators, may concentrate on asking what could possibly authorize the ongoing rhetorical-humanistic imputation of values to things. This is not, for the locals, a trivial question, given that rhetorical transaction, far from automatically placing a seal of approval on whatever exists, typically thrives upon our righteous indignation, our "sense of the ought," our "vision of how matters should go" (Weaver, "Language," 309, 315).

Particularly in the case of Weaver, the "ought" might perhaps be emanating from some Platonic realm of ideality. Yet it's in Weaver's own reference to what is "intimate" about language that we find the more likely rhetorical-humanistic answer, involving a proximate rather than ultimate origin (Weaver, "Language," 316). The intimacy is of a kind obtaining among family and friends, much as in the ancient notion of *oikonomia* (see Eden 1997). It's intrinsic to just the sort of ecumenical economy that makes a household of the entire, expansible flock. But this derivation of agency from the hearthside implies that the rhetorical-humanistic "ought" must be arising from within none other than those intimate, value-laden, conventionally-articulated guidelines which are always already inherited by any bona fide rhetorical agents.

From Normativity to Shared Values

The fact is that rhetorical theorists who appeal to shared values do not often interrogate the genesis of the very guidelines they're invoking. We know this to be the case because, as Calvin O. Schrag (1997) points out, it is an *innovation* for Ramsey and Di Mare, with their "politics of critical rhetoric," to have shown that even "ideals" are mutable, both in themselves and in the effects they promote (74). So the rhetorical-humanistic appeal to collective guidelines, the latter coming from who knows where, does look to be another instance of theoretical fiat, with writers assuring themselves that shared values are necessarily sources of agency simply because they're shared. Yet, in fields quite other than rhetorical studies, as in social theory and cultural theory, commentators have begun arguing, cogently enough, that it may be less important to scrutinize the origin of shared values than to grasp that the shared values, once they're present, can serve as resources helping actors evade normative, indeed oppressive constraints.

We can consider, for the sake of an outside example, the introductory notes which Pisters and Staat provide in *Shooting the Family: Transnational Media and Intercultural Values* (2005). Taking issue with the view of family as a kind of bunker for hegemony (a "backlash resource"), the authors explain that "the intercultural values of migrant families are as particular and contrary to universalist (that is, modernistic) values as natural family values were in the counter-Enlightenment"

(13). For, in "transgressing the borders of the nation-state," these "families make clear that the public realm of nation-state institutions cannot contain the contemporary significance of real families." And so, as in this example concerning the political normativity of the modern(ist) nation-state, commentators from even beyond the discipline of rhetoric are agreeing with the rhetorical-humanistic position, reinforcing its doctrine that the shared, valuated guidelines keeping the group together still don't have to exist in any necessary homology with the hegemonic.

Now, it's conceivable that "norms" and "values" might still be ideological. However, in the rhetorical-humanistic landscape, shared values can only become ideological if they're blended with other elements (objects, aims, ideas, purposes, practices, and the like) to form an ostensibly seamless fabric. Yet shared values, i.e., pure and simple, clearly remain detachable from their contexts. They're not even unconscious, since rhetorical agents can effortlessly draw them to attention, as when arguing that only these, and certainly not those, are the right shared values for the situation.

A case in point is that "patriotism" can prove to be a shared value irreducible to (and de-linkable from) any particular ideology, including among present-day Americans. For there are, evidently, a number of persons who, adhering to "a moral framework that goes back to this nation's founding, and that is inherently progressive," already live "by such principles as service, stewardship, tolerance, and equality of opportunity," showing by example that "devotion to this nation means working to help America reach its exceptional potential and promise" ("Welcome to the True Patriot Network"). In that case, from a rhetorical-humanistic perspective, to say that shared values are ideological wouldn't be accurate. They might be social, cultural, collective, conventional, and so forth, but still without being determinative. And that's exactly as for those true patriots adhering to a moral framework which they declare to be inherently progressive, persons whose stated values it would be quite a stretch to label normative as well.

A Tribe of Equals

When rhetorical transaction is constructed as depending simultaneously on shared human propensities and on shared societal values, it's construed as re-affirming affinity. This preoccupation with like's giving rise to like can explain why rhetorical-humanistic agency is so readily figured as love. An exemplary statement is Richard M. Weaver's "The *Phaedrus* and the Nature of Rhetoric" (1953), with Wayne Brockriede's "Arguers as Lovers" (1972) adding some further nuance. Both take for granted, and both perpetuate, the conviction that rhetorical agency, whenever worthy of its name, necessarily involves the (re)affirmation of a bond between, on the one side, some set of auditors and, on the other side, a rhetor who, in caring for what they value, cares for them as well. For, while the shared values can certainly do the heavy lifting, they cannot lead anyone astray, not here in the rhetorical-humanistic landscape of agency. Instead, any disastrous manipulation, ventriloquation, or zombification must be blamed upon the unworthiness of the interlocutors, especially of the rhetor, who's more than likely mismanaged, if not abused, the freedom to articulate "values" with "things" (Weaver, "Language," 316).

In any case, regardless that the local commentators might consider "bad rhetoric" to be a contradiction in terms, the point remains that, in this world, good rhetoric is efficacious when it is animated by shared values. Yet, eternal as these shared values may appear to be, they are, to the contrary, under constant production, and by agents including the local commentators themselves. That's the explanation as to how such core beliefs, though periodically "forgotten," can so routinely and immediately be remembered, i.e., whenever it's time to close the gap between "existing and desired conditions" (Sheard, qtd. in Villadsen 42).

Let's turn to a couple of contemporary illustrations, good for showing how rhetorical-humanistic theorists can reterritorialize rhetorical conventionality by deploying techniques of consolidation. Such expedients are designed to protect the agency that simply must accrue to shared values in order for rhetorical conventionality to make any difference to speak of.

In his essay on Lincoln's Second Inaugural Address, Hansen (2004) seeks to explain the "endurance" of that certain kind of rhetorical text which is not "exhausted by its situation" (224). He draws on a method of "re-creative criticism," positing that producer and receiver can be linked transhistorically (227). True, "the agency of the producer of the text and its fit audience are mutually dependent, one calling out the other, the absence of one leading to the absence of the other" (230). Nevertheless, any agency worth mentioning must certainly bespeak the continuity between rhetor and audience.

Such continuity would obtain not at the level of some hegemonic subjectivity, but at the level of the more deeply-entrenched values which normativity can only contextualize. For, while "ideologies" may come and go ("coruscating and evolving"), collective values persist (252). Reactivated by features of textual language, style, and form, they establish, in this case, a bridge between Lincoln's neck of the woods and ours. The present-day audience — at least, the part of it that's "fit" — sees past its own provincial ideology, and then the message comes home, animated by the shared values that have been there all along (230).

Interestingly, Hansen speaks not of reconciliation but of revolution: Lincoln's audience, "transformed by the radicalizing knowledge that the speaker has presented," finally "gains new instruments to enact new abilities" (250). At the same time, though, the audience, whether past or present, will be agreeing to just exactly the "instruments" (charity, firmness, self-suppression of malice), and just exactly the goals (unity, peace) which the speaker has been recommending, and these will be thoroughly familiar to the audience, anyway (251). So rhetoric is revolutionary, transformative, and radicalizing not in calling for everything to change, but, instead, in framing "desired" conditions in terms of those familiar, shared values which are always already there, even if they have momentarily "been forgotten" (Sheard, qtd. in Villadsen 42).

Villadsen (2008) analyzes a ceremonial speech aimed at creating a "recommitment to values fit to inspire future collective action" (42). Yet some of the speaker's choices prove to be blunders that "complicate" or undercut his rhetorical agency.

The speech starts functioning as "a site of rhetorical agency for its audiences," who come to understand themselves not as neutral bystanders but as agents who can "partake in an ethical re-evaluation" (40, 43). The most important implication, then, is that rhetorical transaction succeeds when the interlocutors are (in Weaver's terms) imputing the same shared value to the same thing, just as rhetorical transaction falters when they impute that shared value to different things altogether.

For, in Villadsen's case study, the Danish Prime Minister, while apologizing for a former government's collaboration with the Nazis, is applauding the Danish resistance movement for having fought, anyway. By now everyone's remembered the shared values, and no-one disagrees with the imputation of oppression (bad) to the Nazis, or of resistance (good) to the Danish freedom fighters. Then it transpires that the Prime Minister means also to impute "oppression" to an Iraqi regime, and "resistance" to the U.S.-led effort, recently supported by the Prime Minister's own government, to overthrow that dispensation.

Certainly, the same shared values are still in play. The problem is that different (indeed, contextually opposite) objects are now becoming articulated with the shared values, which latter haven't changed at all. From the speaker's perspective, the U.S.-led effort properly articulates with *resistance*. But, as it happens, "many Danes" at this time perceive the "war in Iraq" as "illegal" to begin with, so that, for them, the U.S.-led effort properly articulates with *oppression* (Villadsen 40). This is why they balk, why the rhetorical transaction falters, and why the speaker loses agency. Yet the shared values have simply stayed there, remaining capable of empowering or disempowering just anybody. In fact, the same shared value of resistance both empowers the speaker (when he articulates it with the Danish freedom fighters) and also, albeit by contrast, empowers the audience (when the speaker tries to articulate it with the American forces as well).

So, in the rhetorical-humanistic world, the shared values that are so central to rhetorical agency are not the same as hegemonic norms, for they refer to the desirable rather than the "expected," coming into play *especially* when the expected should not, in fact, prevail (see Barker, 1995). Further, the shared values are accessible to all, regardless of the agents' collectively-determined identities, subject positions, or social roles. And these shared values, as deserves some emphasis, are heterogeneous, rather than homologous. To stipulate valuation X of an object would not, after all, be structurally or functionally equivalent to stipulating valuation Y of that same object. That's why the "many Danes" of whom Villadsen has been writing are left annoyed, not apathetic or impressed, when their Prime Minister shows he can't differentiate between an object properly to be linked with "resistance," and an object properly to be linked with "oppression" (40).

Keeping Shared Values between the Ceiling and the Seat

An important difficulty, from the rhetorical-humanistic perspective, is that the participants in some given transaction might not, at any given moment, be sharing the same values. In that case, theory risks opening the door to a merely relativistic rhetorical agency, that is, of the sort that would exist for those who currently shared the values, but not for those who didn't. Therefore, rhetorical-humanistic commentary (exercising its will to make conventionality matter) has developed a safeguard for ensuring the preponderance of shared values, and, in consequence, for upscaling the reality of the agency that derives from them.

The safeguard, at least conceptually, is to minimize the number of auditors who don't, in fact, share the same values, and to maximize the number of those who do. What this amounts to in practice (and here one means practice as adumbrated by the theorist) is, in effect, the judicious elimination of just as many of the auditors as necessary, leaving in their seats only those who certainly share the same values. We've already witnessed this safeguard in operation. We've discovered that, according to Villadsen, rhetorical agency belongs not merely to those who value resistance over oppression, but to those who value the alignment of each with its proper objects. Similarly, we've seen Hansen, in his essay on Lincoln's Second Inaugural Address, insisting that the audience be "fit" for rhetorical agency — qualified, that is, by its responsiveness to exactly those shared values which underwrite the worthy speaker's message (230).

If we were proceeding as rhetorical-humanistic theorists, we might find it natural to rule out of consideration anyone theoretically unfit to serve as a rhetorical agent. But, since we are proceeding as assemblage-theoretical researchers, our obligation is to scrutinize the collaborative processes by which rhetorical agency is manufactured for distribution. If we look into the support system for theorists like Hansen and Villadsen — technicians bent on spinning rhetoricity directly out of shared values — we'll find the *New Rhetoric* of Perelman and Olbrechts-Tyteca (1958) to be foundational. In fact, that canonical work serves as an instruction manual for leaving in their seats only such auditors as are fit for rhetorical agency.

Here, the salient point of view might appear to be that adopted by the initiating agent. For it's the rhetor who selects, from the options available within the bona fide collectivity, whichever configuration(s) and application(s) of shareable values are parametric for the transaction. On the other hand, everything still rises or falls in accordance with whatever the audience will stand for.

True, "the status of an audience varies with the concepts one has of it," implying that it's primarily the rhetor, the audience rather less so, who determines what the latter would find acceptable (Perelman and Tyteca 34). But if the rhetor could wish herself into speaking before the "universal," or best-possible audience, then she could ignore the stance of any actual audience whatever (Perelman and Tyteca 33). She could dismiss the whole congregation as "recalcitrant," and all on the basis that they didn't actually share the values which the best-possible audience, as she envisioned it, would certainly share. It's exceptional for the rhetor's universal audience to coincide with her actual audience, and she must be careful not to charge too many with recalcitrance. Thus she ought to deploy values lowly enough for even the majority to share, which is again to say that everything turns on the audience's approval.

So the theoretical expedient for maximizing rhetorical agency is two-folded. The rhetor gains agency partly by lowering the ceiling, and partly by raising the floor. For, as Perelman and Tyteca explain, "There can only be adherence to this idea of excluding individuals from the human community" if

> the number and intellectual value of those banned are not so high as to make such a procedure ridiculous. If this danger exists, recourse must be had to another line of argumentation, and the universal audience must be set against an elite audience, endowed with exceptional and infallible means of knowledge. (33)

As necessary, the speaker is to keep dropping her standards to the next-best level, constituting the audience as sharing values just about high or noble enough to make the recommended course of action seem substantive. In this way, she constitutes her audience as fit, as qualified to accede to her own rhetorical agency. And, again as necessary, she constitutes as recalcitrant those hypothetical auditors unlikely to meet even the lowered level of expectation.

That's how the rhetorical-humanistic speaker so often manages to make things otherwise than they are. Picking her battles wisely, she argues for the value of altering the present dispensation by just enough, but never too much. She shores up her own agency by imputing recalcitrance, not to mention imbecility, to any hypothetical auditor who'd undervalue this indisputably moderate, though still desirable degree of change. Meanwhile, both the ground floor and the ceiling are projections from the value-set which the rhetor always already shares with the bona fide community, with the result that the transaction only ever takes place among those who are welcome at the familial hearthside.

We now see that it's theoretically possible for rhetorical conventionality to transform rhetorical subjectivity itself, as when shared values enable a speaker situationally to redraw the boundary between the "fit" and the "recalcitrant" (Hansen 230; Perelman and Tyteca 33). In the rhetorical-humanistic world, "terms" — here, with reference to shared values — can exceed any "relations" in which they're temporarily embedded, which is to say that social structures, significations, subject positions are not *internalized* constraints, but "external" to the values traveling through them (Baugh 36; Colebrook 5). In addition, the rhetorical-humanistic paradigm not only illustrates but even operationalizes the synergy obtaining between "reterritorialization" and "deterritorialization" (Palmås 3). Rhetorical agents can reterritorialize rhetorical conventionality by conceptually banishing those who don't share the same values. Consequently, they can deterritorialize rhetorical subjectivity, stretching it out with the aid of those standards that are indeed held in common by the remaining interlocutors.

Staying the Same by Doing Something Differently

Returning, even while we're here in the rhetorical-humanistic world, to the Sojourner Truth literature, we can start seeing how an exemplary practitioner could parley the topics of *race, gender, work, mind, biblical precept,* and *embodiment,* together with a certain metaphor about the pint and the quart, into a means of transforming the sorts of interiority prevalent within the status quo. In this case, the agents of change happen to include certain shared values. They facilitate the emergence of an alternative way of knowing and acting, such that the interlocutors can agree on the justice of granting to the disenfranchised, or at least to one or two sub-sets of them, the same legal rights as any other bona fide members of the collectivity. But, in that case, the famous speech of 1851, rather than attempting to frame the natural rights as already formidable (i.e., in the social-structural manner considered earlier) must be attempting precisely the opposite. It must be portraying the natural rights as languishing in exile, such that its own function becomes to bring them back into the familial fold.

In nineteenth-century America, natural rights are as familiar as legal rights, though the two kinds of rights are, at this moment, in contradiction. To resolve the contradiction requires the adjustment of legal rights until they are consistent with natural rights. Yet this will be the *alteration* of the status quo, taking place through the reconciliation of a presently hegemonic discourse (that of legal rights) with a presently marginalized discourse (that of natural rights). Such a reconciliation can take place if the two discourses are rendered commensurable, as on the basis of any values shared by the adherents to the discourses themselves.

Again, it's the task of the whole person — at least, when she's acting as rhetor — to speak in a manner that, manifesting love, shifts the collectivity back to the future. For, in helping us recollect the shared values that have always kept us together, the exemplary rhetorical practitioner helps us adapt. She helps us become otherwise than we are, and precisely so that we can stay lovable (albeit, from now on, a little more so than of late). To do that, she constitutes herself as a docent, someone who helps us revisit, remember, reinterpret our shared values, so that we come to see for ourselves the "disparity between existing and desired conditions," the mismatch that, before our very eyes, becomes "the subject of critique" (Sheard, qtd. in Villadsen 42). This docent will indeed serve as a kind of lover, just as in Weaver (1953) or Brockriede (1972). Yet she may as well serve as a teacher, a guide, a parent.

In both the Gage and Robinson versions of the speech, this agency of the docent is manifested wherever the speaker frames her audience as children. The underlying appeal, ostensibly from maternal authority, isn't to sassify the speaker: O, that authentic Sojourner Truth, so down-home and so country! Instead, it's to reassure, and to comfort, and to inculcate trust. Let's recognize, therefore, that "children" is a rhetorical-humanistic technique — not too different from, say, "Four score and seven years ago." It's a transition, much like a cinematic wipe, but placing us within earshot of an interpreter, of someone who recovers and reminds us about our collective values. Of course, just about anybody in our community may need such reminding. But, then again, just about anybody can act as docent.

For the reminder doesn't have to come from some credential-bearing specialist; it's not a question of scholastic training or fancy paraphernalia. To the contrary, the reminder can come from just any speaker who's remembered the familiar, ecumenical guidelines, those that can help her decrease the space between ceiling and floor.

Now, it's true that, in the rhetorical-humanistic landscape, an appeal to "common values, undisputed though not formulated," can only be made "by one who is qualified to do so" (Perelman and Tyteca 53). But this isn't so exclusionary a requirement as it may sound. The docent gets to be qualified in the same, perfectly manageable way as does the docent's beneficiary: by clearly *not* being "recalcitrant" (Perelman and Tyteca 33). This means that the rhetorical agent is anyone whose values are the same as ours. And if it happens that she's just as comfortable in her impromptu role as in her own skin, i.e., in her possession of the Standard Human Complement, then so much the better for the recovery of our collective values.

In the rhetorical-humanistic world, the docent can always draw upon certain local conventions, for example, of genre. But even the genre-conventions will be perfectly accessible. Certainly, the nineteenth-century rhetor might invoke the time-binding powers of narrative. That'd be a way of universalizing what's all too easily mistaken for a regional contingency — as with the famous opening for Lincoln's Gettysburg Address. But, then again, she might as readily appropriate the genre conventions of the come-all-ye, that populist sort of utterance to reappear, so much later, in the songs of Woody Guthrie: "Well, gather 'round me, children, a story I will tell / 'bout Pretty Boy Floyd the outlaw, Oklahoma knew him well."

Always, though, the message rests between shared values, those which the docent has bolted into place, forming upper and lower brackets for the problem confronting the group:

> As through this life you ramble
> As through this life you roam
> You'll never see an outlaw
> Drive a family from their home.

So the shared values that the docent invokes will not have to do with any pre-determined social identity, essence, or station in life. They won't even have to do with the currently privileged medium of communication, not so long as story exceeds the provenance of alphanumeric text. This is precisely why nobody who inhabits a world like the rhetorical-humanistic would ever find it paradoxical for an "old, illiterate, former slave woman" to be acting as a docent, as a bona fide rhetorical agent (Campbell 9).

Maximizing Assent by Minimizing Recalcitrance

The technical use of "children" tells us we're in the presence of someone activating what is axiomatically conventional about rhetoricity — in this case, by bringing collective values into the transaction. But the docent won't bring in just any collective values, only those which are suited to the situation. For we, the undecided auditors, do need to undertake some self-modification, as by returning (from our idiosyncratic preoccupations) to our communal roots. Indeed, it's in recalling just those few collective guidelines which we'd forgotten, and in reviewing them under the tutelage of the docent who loves us, that we're to become otherwise than we are, though remaining lovable all the while. And that, the assemblage-theoretical investigator should conclude, must be why Sojourner Truth isn't actually asserting the rightfulness of "natural rights," pure and simple, let alone the wrongfulness of say, social, political, or legal rights as presently constituted. For to valorize natural rights over everything else would be to insinuate that the American republic must be unlovable by design.

In the middle of the nineteenth century, to hew too closely to a natural-rights position would be to shift the focus from what binds us to what divides us, the divisive reality, in this particular instance, being that of class. Admittedly, Sojourner Truth does hint, in both the Gage and the Robinson versions of her speech, at how often she (as the representative of an entire constituency) has been left hungry. She'll "eat" as much as she can "get," but that doesn't mean she always gets enough to eat (Painter, Sojourner Truth, 125; Campbell 10). Still, it's possible, even in the rhetorical-humanistic landscape of agency, that the unfortunate might be so for any number of reasons; and, in any case, the speaker isn't betraying the least suggestion that slavery and/or women's subjugation, or even exploitation based on class, might be wrong in principle.

That would be precisely the kind of argument, the argument from ideality, that we should expect to hear from any purism of natural rights: some set of claims to the effect that slavery, women's subjugation, and class exploitation are inherently wrongful. But there's nothing along those lines in the Robinson version of the speech, and this, as we've noted in an earlier connection, would appear to be a remarkable omission on the part of someone who'd been tarred and feathered for the ardency of his own natural-rights abolitionism. Meanwhile, there's nothing like it in the Gage version, either, regardless that the latter does imply there to be some "rights" which "are not conferred but inhere in persons" (Campbell 10).

So what could be the rationale for the speaker's outright avoidance of the least suggestion that slavery, sexual subjugation, exploitation of the subalterns by the elites, might be wrong in principle? Well, the answer is that, while everyone in the audience can accept that some of their practices may call for revision, not everyone can accept that some of their principles may need revision too. If the speaker is refraining from asserting the supremacy of natural rights, pure and simple, that's because she knows better than to advocate a morally unimpeachable stance which would, for that very reason, be politically untenable.

Thus, if we do triangulate (looking to the intersection where Robinson and Gage agree), we'll notice just how cautious is Sojourner Truth, as she dwells on the topics of work, biblical precept and mind, to skirt the topics of property, dispossession, and class. Still, it's precisely because shared values are heterogeneous, strategically separable, that they can be deployed, rather like the croupier's rake, for finessing auditors into the familiar fold. Indeed, the speaker can gather up any number of auditors, just so long as these do not bring along with them the sharable value of ownership. That's very much as we've seen above, where Perelman and Olbrechts-Tyteca do emphasize that any rhetor must be circumspect enough to lower her standards when necessary.

As an exemplary rhetorical agent, Sojourner Truth would recognize that to associate ownership with recalcitrance would be to banish from the conversation the majority of her own (actual, and perhaps even potential) auditors, indeed, practically everyone but the slave and the pauper. For, according to the rhetorical-humanistic perspective, rhetoric does come into its own by offering something for everybody, that is, for everybody who shares the same values. But there wouldn't be something for everybody in a jeremiad on exploitation — whether on that of the factory worker by the industrialist, or on that of the wife by the master of the house, or on that of the domestic servant by the wife herself. Ownership, property, class: these would only separate us, and, if the point is to keep us together, then why bring them up at all? So, the speaker can hardly be expected to pitch her appeals at the loftiest level imaginable, as by asking the auditors to indict themselves for their complicity in economic, sexual, and racial exploitation. Instead, she can be expected to invoke some lowlier criteria than that, leaving almost all the auditors in their seats, but giving them something to rise for, too.

Thus we come to see the docent as appealing not to the taintless, unimpeachable values of an ideal audience but to the relatively more humble values of an "elite" audience (Perelman and Tyteca 34). The elite audience in this case simply consists of those whose "knowledge" is at least "exceptional" and "infallible" enough for them to know the value of work, and of biblical precept, and of mind. If it happens that Sojourner Truth's elite-enough audience additionally subscribes to values conducing to class exploitation, dispossession, and the like, then that's truly unfortunate. But it's still no reason not to grab onto any handles available for aligning listeners with their better natures, if not absolutely their best. Besides, an audience that can be constituted as valuing work, biblical precept, and mind is also an audience ready to recall that all of these do lie at the very intersection between natural rights and legal rights.

Let's therefore consider that, if the Sojourner Truth speech does emphasize the hard work that our docent, or persons like her, have already performed, then this is not a self-advertising of physical prowess but a verification that the presently-marginalized do share the work ethic already valued by the speaker's audience. For who but a social-structural theorist could think that the rhetorical agent, in arguing for equality of rights, must also be arguing that she is naturally built for all of this back-breaking labor, in other words, perfectly suited to her structural role?

Instead, the speaker is showing that she, like those for whom she speaks, understands very well that it's only work, not something disturbing like ownership, which is at issue now. It's this appreciation of the value of work, this cognizance of the obligation to help make the social world go round (as Nell Irvin Painter says, in the way of "production," "transportation," and "consumption") that unifies the speaker — indeed, her rights-less constituency — with an undecided audience positioned to make a difference (*Sojourner Truth* 126–27). So the examples from personal experience are there to argue for "equality of opportunity" not by invoking natural rights, but by invoking the work ethic that just any auditor would share, other than, of course, in cases of recalcitrance (Campbell 10).

Even the integration of biblical precept becomes articulated with the shared value of work, though in a manner perhaps more pointed for the historical audience than for the present day social-structural theorist. To be sure, in both the Robinson and the Gage versions of the speech, the speaker does refer to all the agricultural labor — plowing, reaping, husking, chopping, and mowing — that she's done during her life. Nevertheless, it's still the case, and in Robinson's version of the speech as much as in Gage's, that "work" is allied with "biblical precept" as well. So let's examine the rhetorical process through which "work" starts traveling in the company of "biblical precept" — with "class" coming along, albeit invisibly, for the ride.

As Nell Irvin Painter acknowledges, while the historical Sojourner Truth contributed lots of "household work" (laundering, cooking, cleaning) in reciprocation to the various activist families with whom she "stayed for extended periods," that's simply not the kind of labor the rhetorical Sojourner Truth chooses to thematize (*Sojourner Truth* 126). Instead, our exemplary practitioner emphasizes "the work of the farm," which she, "along with masses of other Americans, including other rural women," idealizes "as the embodiment of real work." Yet we really shouldn't stop there, i.e., with Painter's historical-biographical suggestion that Sojourner Truth might be serving as yet another spokesperson for nineteenth-century pastoralism.

For what's more rhetorically important is that the work of the farm (ontologically preceding any laundering, cooking, cleaning) is an activity from which all Americans benefit. It's an activity in which many of them have first-hand experience, and, in any case, it's an activity which most of them, not counting the recalcitrant, are likely to value. That's the explanation for a folk song like the following, from Sojourner Truth's own era, though circulated more widely during the populist movements of the 1890s:

> You may talk of all the nobles of the earth
> Of the kings who hold the nations in their thrall
> Yet in this we all agree, if we only look and see
> That the farmer is the man that feeds us all.

It's back-breaking labor, yes. But at least it's a sunny kind of backbreaking labor — and you'd be the salt of the earth if you knew it. For farm work really does offer something for everyone.

In short, there's nothing more reconciliatory than to celebrate the sorts of "real work" through which we Americans do earn our keep, putting our rightfully-won bread on the family table (Painter, *Sojourner Truth*, 126). And just any non-recalcitrant auditor can sense that this work ethic (bespeaking authentic labor — the effort, for example, of those who do reap and sow and gather into barns, as in that passage from Matthew to which Sojourner Truth alludes in her speech) must be shared universally. That's why so much of the speech would be about farming, in this way recalling the better part of the audience to its traditional family values.

What's just as evident, though, is that Sojourner Truth is definitely citing scripture, since she's doing so not only in Gage but also in Robinson. From this perspective, we can again see that Gage and Robinson are together drawing our attention to the rhetorical-humanistic agency that accrues to shared values.

4 :: CONVENTIONALITY IN THE RHETORICAL-HUMANISTIC LANDSCAPE | 93

They're doing so whenever they report on Sojourner Truth's incorporation into the speech of any Judeo-Christian references at all.

For the function of such references wouldn't be to furnish the speaker with some theological or supernatural warrant in support of political enfranchisement. Instead, it would be to bring into the forum certain reminders of the shared, deeply-entrenched values which are keeping speaker and audience connected. True, it's only in Gage that we find a line like this:

> I have borne thirteen chilern, and seen 'em mos' all sold off to slavery, and when I cried out with [sic] my mother's grief, none but Jesus heard me! (Campbell 10)

But if we only look and see, we'll recognize that the point isn't to perseverate on what the speaker "has done as a woman and suffered as a mother" (10). To the contrary, it's to establish the speaker's ethos as someone whose scriptural values saturate her to the core. She remains bound to Jesus, even when the rest of us have forgotten that she actually shares our faith. Indeed, it's her own faith, authenticated with each of her citations of a Judeo-Christian commonplace, that constitutes her as consubstantial with us. And then there's no longer any reason for the other family members, those who aren't recalcitrant, to wonder about any fundamental disparity between the speaker's values and their own.

At this stage, we should be fairly clear as to how it is that "work" and "biblical precept" can, by way of shared values, become sources of rhetorical agency — the sort that translates convention into a means of altering sociality. It's worth noting in this connection that the shared values can also fold race and gender, maybe even "embodiment," into all the rest of the American collectivity. For all we have to do is open our eyes and look at who's expressing these shared values, here at this woman's rights convention of 1851. But what remains to be addressed is the topic of "mind," together with the complex metaphor of the pint and the quart, a figure which itself proves consistent with the shared values of "work" and "biblical precept."

Again, given that we have shifted to the rhetorical-humanistic landscape, we will understand that what makes it possible for social realities to change, to emerge or come into being, is that the present dispensation can always be redeemed through the common language established by shared values. This lingua franca can even translate the discourse of natural rights into commensurability with the discourse of legal rights. Thus, if we do turn to the rhetorical-humanistic uses of "mind," we'll find that the Sojourner Truth speech must be invoking yet another shared value, that which accrues to none other than reasoned debate. This latter, of course, is "conventional" in that it's just how we nineteenth-century Americans ordinarily go about negotiating our collective destiny.

Earlier, during the course of a social-structural reading of the pint-and-quart analogy, we've come to see that, in the middle of the nineteenth century, the discourse of natural rights cannot, in isolation, count for very much, what with its already being trumped by a discourse indisputably more normative than itself. Nevertheless, there is still a way to bridge the discourse of natural rights with the discourse of, say, legal rights. Let's recall that the political rationale for the republic has always been to uphold an alternative to government by arbitrary power. This alternative is validated by the people's right publicly to discuss, revise, and select from the options available in the marketplace of ideas. Thus, even in the United States of Sojourner Truth's day, the shared value of deliberation is hybridized, on the one side, with the discourse of natural rights and, on the other side, with the discourse of civil, or social, or statutory rights. The metaphor of the pint and the quart can capitalize upon both sorts of discourse simultaneously. It's a reminder that reason isn't, after all, a zero-sum game (everybody can have as much of it as they naturally do, without depleting anyone else's), and it's also a reminder that reason itself supplies an irrefragable justification for altering the present dispensation.

So here's a rhetorical-humanistic gloss of the metaphor in question, a gloss which, rather than having primarily to do with guilt, craniometry, physique, essence, or parody, has primarily to do with the shared value of reasoned debate. Sojourner Truth is saying that even if she and the members of her constituency were (naturally) endowed with a smaller-than-optimal amount of reason, their reason, whether it were measured by pint or by quart, would be reason nonetheless. Meanwhile, as everybody knows, this American experiment is such that superior, quart-sized reasons have incessantly to earn their keep by vanquishing inferior, pint-sized reasons. Since so many among the disenfranchised must possess at least some rationality, it's no less than a political failure to discount their potential contributions, in other words, to rule out these same untapped reservoirs of reason, some of which might yet turn out to be quart-sized, after all.

Certainly, it makes good practical sense for us, the undecided auditors, to help expand the range of enfranchisement. As it is, we already appreciate the value of real work. So we just need to remember that intellectual labor is another of the practices that keep the nation humming along. In addition, there's nothing for us to lose in emancipating at least one or two subsets of the currently marginalized. Should any among them, making their way into the public forum, betray their half-measured inferiority, that will just give us something to argue all the way back to the farm, the domicile, the factory. It's how American democracy operates: by pitting the better arguments against the worse. Meanwhile, if any among the newly-enfranchised turn out to be competent, there will still be no problem. For this, too, is what it means for the better arguments to win. Besides, since reason is the currency of the political marketplace, it's clear that statutory (or legal, or civil) rights are to be earned, indeed purchased through reasoned debate. In that case, to persist in silencing certain intellects on the basis of race or gender is to persist in vitiating the political process. It's as inimical to the spirit of the republic as price-fixing would be to the spirit of free enterprise.

By now, we've indeed come upon a way to frame rhetorical agency as "conventional," though without necessitating its pollution by normativity. In this extended example, the shared values accorded to work, biblical precept, and mind do return the collectivity to a certain equilibrium, yet they do not function in a manner that can be called merely conservative. Rather, they effect what is simultaneously a reconciliation and a transformation. By linking alternative discourses, they promote inclusion and enfranchisement. And, in broadening the range of the ecumenical family, they help the collectivity remain itself by becoming otherwise, as by welcoming into the fold certain constituencies which, up to now, have (irrationally) been excluded from the household.

Still Missing So Far

As we've seen, the rhetorical-humanistic perspective explains rhetorical agency in terms of the deployment of shared values. Thus theory supports (rather than undermines) practice, for it frames collectively held guidelines as resources for reconfiguring rhetorical subjectivity. Yet the reterritorialization of rhetorical conventionality does require the elevation of certain values at the expense of others. For instance, as we've seen above, democratization might carefully be sutured to the value of work, biblical precept, and mind, but just as carefully amputated from the value of ownership, property, and cash money. This implies that rhetoric's (Heideggerian) saving power might very well be founded upon no less than its exploitative danger. And the only rhetorical-humanistic defense for such duplicity seems to be that it is actually the rhetor's duty to promote the greater good by whatever means are available.

To bring the duplicity more clearly into view, we'll give it a face, acknowledging its likely impact on any human actors caught up in rhetorical transaction. So let's consider the opinion of Emmanuel Lévinas, who, even as a philosopher of communication, denies that there's any justification for rhetoric at all. Citing Plato's *Phaedrus* as an illustration, Lévinas maintains that the "specific nature of rhetoric" is to inculcate "propaganda, flattery, diplomacy," indeed, to effect "psychagogy, demagogy, pedagogy" (70). In short, rhetorical transaction looks to be all "ruse, emprise, and exploitation" (72). Although Lévinas provides only the most cursory analysis, his complaint still poses a problem quite devastating for the tradition, a tradition in which Plato himself is continually tortured into admitting that, but of course, rhetoric's true purpose is to uphold the (universally) greater good.

After all, while the *Phaedrus* does take the form of a dialogue, on the question of a true art of rhetoric, the true art uncovered there isn't dialogic. According to Plato's Socrates, the best of all possible rhetoricians will aspire to understanding things exactly as they are — aspire, that is, to grasping a "being that really is what it is" (Plato 33). So, once the requisite teleology establishes the frame for everything else, the task degenerates into audience analysis, also known as homework. But, in that case, rhetorical utterance isn't conversation, it's indoctrination. It's to regroup the audience under the sign of the given, the unalterable, the "being that really is what it is." There's no provision in the true art of rhetoric for protecting, only for co-opting, the otherness of the interlocutor. And this, for Lévinas, is what counts as psychagogy, demagogy, and pedagogy.

It's difficult to refute Lévinas by asserting that, no, regardless of what Plato or Socrates might say about the authoritarian, top-down trajectory of, frankly, even the most truly rhetorical communication, rhetoric is still, by and large, quite open to radical alterity. The basic criticism obviously applies to any rhetoric addressing its auditors "in the name of their highest good" (Weaver, "Language," 309). For the Lévinasian indictment is correct: the rhetorical-humanistic tendency is to submit, indeed, to betray the person to the group. Under these circumstances, while there's a social rationale for speech, there isn't a human justification at all.

5.
Transcendence in the Existential-Transversal Landscape

FORTUNATELY FOR CONTEMPORARY rhetorical theory (given the implications of the Lévinasian critique) there's still one kind of value that acts in tension with, rather than in subservience to, the greater good. It concerns the non-finessable, non-negotiable, indeed *non-rational* claim of every human being upon a free, authentic, and responsible existence. To understand the sort of agency that could accrue to such a claim, we'll visit a place where theorists are continually (re)territorializing rhetoric's power to make things otherwise. According to the locals, rhetoric's productivity, or efficacy, belongs to an agent whose very manner of being is emergent. That's why, in this third landscape of agency, a claim like "I am a woman's rights" will be heard as valorizing the "am."

Existence, Transcendence, and Transversality

Some rhetorical-theoretical investigators have pursued the senses in which responsibility (Schrag, 1997), conscience (Hyde, 1994), and questioning (Turnbull, 2004) all become sites of rhetorical transcendence. For these writers, responsibility, conscience, and questioning are among not the potential, but the actual and inalienable affordances available to what might be called — here to borrow again from Anton and Peterson (2003) — the *existential self*. This latter, as implied in the work of, say, Georges Gusdorf (1965), Hans Blumenberg (1987), or Ernesto Grassi (2001), is by now presupposed in projects like that of Thomas Rickert (2013).

Since "existentialism" is a constituent of the stance in question, we'll note that this is a philosophy according to which existence precedes essence, with existence understood not as a prior category but as a "self-making-in-a-situation" (Fackenheim 37). However, existentialism additionally holds that "human beings came into existence through natural, evolutionary processes, and then created myths and religious beliefs to explain their unique importance" (Hall 132). Of course, the term "natural" implies "contingent" rather than "inevitable," since existentialist writers are likely to include biological determinism among the "myths" to be rejected. Even so, if *vitalism* is the assertion that life exceeds reduction to the pre-determined, to the mechanistic, then existentialism ought to be vitalism, too — and presumably occasionalism as well. What's crucial, after all, is the contrast whereby existence proceeds from life, but essence from social determination. Therefore, existentialism, insofar as it does tie human existence to "evolutionary processes," should probably consider the *sine qua non* of this existence to be our living materiality as such.

However, in preparation for an upcoming local pitfall — namely, the existential-transversal forgetfulness of materiality — let's proceed by consulting some existentialism proper, that is, with reference to the work of Jean-Paul Sartre's close ally, Simone de Beauvoir. In *The Ethics of Ambiguity* (1948), Beauvoir argues that the only absolute value is that of existence, willed into being whenever we take a stand in favor of the life-affirming over against the life-denying. Thus Beauvoir illustrates the way in which transcendence can be said to remain ontologically independent of everything else. For she presents "freedom" as a recurrent return "to the positive," a return which gives existence "a content through action, escape, political struggle, revolution: Human transcendence then seeks, with the destruction of the given situation, the whole future which will flow from its victory" (31). Clearly, this transcendence involves an *endless* breaking-up of whatever social conditions are currently in place.

From a generally existentialist viewpoint, it's always that "man must…assume," i.e., both posit and embrace, "his finiteness: not by treating his existence as transitory or relative but by reflecting the infinite within it, that is, by treating it as absolute" (Beauvoir 130–31). Yet there are cases in which freedom takes on a negative or reactive complexion. For, while "liberation" is "a movement" which "realizes itself by tending to conquer," action cannot "seek to fulfill itself by means which would destroy its very meaning" (131). Thus, in "certain situations there will be no other issue for man than rejection." Such rejection might include militancy, "action," "political struggle," "revolution." But it will always contrast with "political realism," where everything is compromise — precisely as in that viewpoint on rhetorical agency where shared values do, in manufacturing the greater good, keep trumping the freedom of any group member.

After all, there is genuine, transcendent "rejection only if man lays claim in the present to his existence as an absolute value," in which case "he must absolutely reject what would deny this value" (Beauvoir 131). Nowadays, as the author explains, that is, "in the name of such an ethics," we'd "condemn" all those Vichyites who were trying "to make the best of things," for that ought to have been a matter not of "rationalizing the present such as it was imposed by the German occupation," but of "rejecting it unconditionally":

> The resistance did not aspire to a positive effectiveness; it was a negation, a revolt, a martyrdom; and in this negative movement freedom was positively and absolutely confirmed. (131)

So, regardless that political realism does look synonymous with existentialist suicide, transcendent agency must still, on this view, be conceptualized as ethical, though in the way of the *authentic* rather than the socially-determined.

For example, in the illustration provided by Beauvoir, we can be sure that, once upon a time, appeasement really did constitute the most rational if least authentic course of action. For, if such an expedient could ever have made sense, that would have been after reality itself had proven unreasonable, as when a certain Vichyite commonsensicality and a certain Nazi irrationality were co-constructing a "state of affairs" just as real as it could be (Schrag 91). As for us today, if we were to collect enough such cases of local (dis)ordering, we'd be confronted with the universal principle underlying them all — which is that, as one of our own contemporaries has observed, there's an "absence of reason inherent in everything" (Meillassoux 53). Under the circumstances, all that's left, as an alternative to the abyss, is our incalculably human claim to life, to an authentically free and responsible, if also counter-rational existence.

It's no surprise that the rhetorical theorist Calvin Schrag (henceforth treated as an ambassador for the existential-transversal position) would wish to draw so bright a distinction between, on the one side, responsitivity and, on the other side, responsibility. To the extent that we're managing to get by, negotiating our pragmatic "being-with-others," we're best described as responsive (Schrag 91). But we shift into genuine responsibility by adopting an insistently "ethical stance" — that which is, more properly, "an *ethos*, a way of dwelling in a social world that gives rise to human goals and purposes, obligations, duties, and concerns for human rights."

Yet, as investigators, we should further contextualize Schrag's affirmation of responsibility by considering the manner in which existentialism proper would explain the origins of transcendence. It would frame transcendence as arising not out of, say, the agent's capacity for rational deliberation, much less out of any traditions the agent may have inherited, but, rather, out of *nowhere*: out of an inexplicable motivation for exceeding whatever there is.

After all, the claim to life, arising in what Beauvoir calls "the original helplessness from which man surges up," must itself be what generates the existential imperatives otherwise missing from the world — including the ethical stance to which Schrag refers as responsibility (Beauvoir 12). For, building on Sartre, Beauvoir notes that there's "no external justification" whatever for this self-warranting claim upon existence: "no outside appeal, no objective necessity permits of its being called useful. It has no reason to will itself. But this does not mean that it can not justify itself, that it can not *give itself* reasons for being that it does not *have*." This is a way of saying that the transcendent claim to a free, responsible existence is prior to everything, preceding any social overlay that could ever come to mask it.

So, in treating Schrag as exemplifying the existential-transversal perspective, and in tracing his discussion of transcendence back to its support system, we can begin to see that rhetorical transcendence is being constructed, on the one side, as if it's anchored in nothing (arising from nowhere), but then, on the other side, as if it's anchored in Sartrean philosophy. And now that we have a stronger sense of what's "existential" about Schrag's position, we can turn to what's "transversal" about it.

Transversality, at least in its Sartrean variety, is the construct which rhetorical theorists like Schrag (and, more implicitly, Michael Hyde or Nick Turnbull) are invoking whenever they imply that transcendence must be operationalized exclusively within consciousness, where it creates "unity" as "a coefficient" of all "thought and communication" (Schrag 129). And Jean-Paul Sartre — as the author of *The Transcendence of the Ego: An Existentialist Theory of Consciousness* (1937) — is indeed among the philosophers to whom such rhetorical theorists continue pledging fealty: "it was the genius of Sartre to recognize" that "consciousness achieves unification by dint" of a built-in "transversal function, an extending across and revisiting of past moments of consciousness without solidifying into an identification with any particular moment" (Schrag 128-129). So, on this account, transversality becomes the royal road for rhetorical transcendence, the latter traveling epistemically.

Schrag, for his own part, seeks to validate this rather subjectivist train of thought by also appealing to another sort of transversality, that to be found in Félix Guattari's *Molecular Revolution: Psychiatry and Politics* (1984). Yet there is a pivotal distinction between the transversality theorized by Sartre and the transversality theorized by Guattari. Since Schrag overlooks the distinction, we should note that Guattari is actually talking about the interaction between subjective and non-subjective resources, so that his version of transversality bespeaks a linkage between minds and non-minds — not only, as in Sartre, between minds and minds. Guattari's conception of transversality arises from his critique of "transference," that psychoanalytic way of explaining how feelings and desires are redirected (3). But, in Guattari's view, transference has become a tool of the status quo. It perpetuates normativity through impositions from above, as well as through institution-wide inertia, such that it forces "things and people" to "fit in as best they can with the situation in which they find themselves" (17). By contrast, "transversality" denotes a "dimension" that may "overcome both the impasse of pure verticality and mere horizontality," as by permitting "maximum communication among different levels and, above all, in different meanings" (18).

Perhaps Guattari's transversality does so closely resemble Sartre's as to explain how an existential-transversal insider could miss the distinction. Yet, from an outsider's point of view, Guattari's emphasis on the non-conscious, non-determined, and non-representational aspects of transversality sticks out like, well, a sore thumb. For Guattari argues that the "best safeguard" against the "danger" of normalization is "to bring to the surface" not, for example, the group's brightest ideas, but, here in a phrase invoking Marx, Freud, and Darwin simultaneously, the group's "instinctual demands" (21). These latter, in requiring "everyone" to "consider the problem of their being and destiny," can render any group (or institution) "ambiguous." In some respects, the collectivity does remain "reassuring and protective, screening all access to transcendence, generating…a mode of alienation one cannot help finding comforting." At the same time, though, "there appears behind this artificial reassurance the most detailed picture of human finitude, in which every undertaking of mine [becomes] caught up in the existence of the other, who alone guarantees what reaches me via human speech."

A passage like that may sound life-affirming in precisely the style of Sartre, of Beauvoir, of Lévinas. Yet "instinctual demands" (which Guattari here associates with our transversal "access to transcendence") turn out to evade social determination altogether. They inhere in that which is irreducible: our materiality, our corporeality, our embodiment. For Guattari, as a matter of fact, transcendence informs the transversal movement from one presence, regardless how finite, to another. By contrast, Sartrean (and, by extension, existential-transversal) transcendence is so immaterial as to be making its way exclusively among absences, that is, entirely within the "no-thing" which Sartre proclaims consciousness to be (Zahavi 136).

Actually, during our visit to the existential-transversal landscape, we have so far been examining the local production of rhetorical transcendence in an *ontological* sense — the way in which it's theorized as inherent to every existential self. Now we'll consider the local manufacture of rhetorical transcendence in a *methodological* sense — the way in which it's theorized as an intra-psychic sub-routine.

Thus we reach a fork in the road. Whereas the ontological explanation derives from Sartrean existentialism (declaring that transcendence is prior to everything), the methodological explanation, by contrast, derives from Sartrean phenomenology (whispering that transcendence must remain contingent upon subjectivity). Taking quite the wrong turn, though purely for investigative purposes, we'll follow the local theorists of rhetorical agency as they drop right into the rabbit-hole of human interiority. While we're in free-fall (through a chamber still echoing with ever so many rumors about the subject's discursive construction), we, too, may begin to wonder why even transcendence shouldn't be socially determined, after all.

Philosophizing for the Living by Getting Rid of Their Materiality

Unfortunately, what Sartre is offering rhetorical theory with the one, existentialist hand is the same as what he's taking away with the other, phenomenologist hand. He's observing, as is well known, that social productions are to be overcome when they exacerbate the material constraints upon human freedom. But then he's insisting they're to be overcome through the force of an interiority lacking in any material dimension at all. To grasp that the project of the existential Sartre is trivialized in the project of the phenomenological Sartre, we'll review the steps through which the latter repurposes such tenets as he's taken over from Edmund Husserl. For Sartre proposes to bring philosophy back to earth by etherealizing it. As a result, it's a retro-fitted, de-corporealized kind of phenomenology, carried over from Sartre, which the existential-transversal theorists are now parlaying into the study of rhetorical transcendence.

Husserl's major contribution, reportedly, is to have opened the way to the things themselves. But his first step has been to get rid of the things themselves, lest they complicate his opening the way to them. So he brackets all "questions of fact," even questions concerning the "evidence for one's own existence as a particular person" (Williams and Kirkpatrick 16–17). Husserl is then addressing only the "intended" or "intentional" objects of consciousness. These are always *thoughts* figured as objects, without regard to whether they correspond to anything existing independently of the thinker. Indeed, the "things" to which Husserl refers are, in every respect, inherent to "the content of a person's thought" (Coates). And then Sartre remains "essentially in agreement" with the "phenomenological program" as laid out by Husserl (Williams and Kirkpatrick 17). He takes for granted, in other words, that the category of "object" is exclusively filled out by objects of intention. All he discards is the Husserlian premise that there's some sort of transcendental ego whose task is to intend the objects themselves.

But what else, if not an "I," shall there be to intend all those objects? Sartre's response is to point out that the question would block the way to the answer:

> nothing shall constitute contents of consciousness into intended objects, for the important reason that consciousness has no contents. All content is on the side of the object. Consciousness contains neither transcendental ego nor anything else. It is simply a spontaneity, a sheer activity transcending toward objects…a great emptiness, a wind blowing toward objects. (Williams and Kirkpatrick 20–21)

In that case, however, the hard-boiled Sartre, the one rolling up his sleeves against the "practico-inert," must be saying the opposite of what the Husserlian Sartre has in mind (see Campbell 4).

Sure, if the objects are already there, with all of the content on their side, then that sounds like a version of philosophical realism: objects are real, and objects are everything. Meanwhile, if consciousness is content-less, then that sounds like a refutation of subjectivism. Yet the only objects that can possibly be left in the picture are *intended* objects, in short, ideas. So, if ideas are everything, and if they're already there, then this is, in fact, idealism, and quite the subjectivist idealism at that. Thus we arrive at the explanation as to why these existential-transversal theorists of rhetorical agency, having founded their views upon a no-thing inherited from Sartre, would keep forgetting that human embodiment does count for something, anyway.

The Two Styles of Transcendence

It's no wonder that, in the tradition following from Sartre, *everything* looks immanent to subjectivity. True, "immanence" is regularly contrasted with "transcendence," as if these are mutually exclusive or diametrically opposed. Yet writers such as Schrag, Hyde, and Turnbull do understand, and all too well, that transcendence itself can be described as immanent: as enclosed within consciousness. So these existential-transversal theorists, what with their belonging to an assemblage for shoring up rhetorical transcendence, are faced with an embarrassing predicament. Given their commitment to life (existence, authenticity, responsibility, and the like) they have to keep showing that speech really can make things otherwise. Then again, given their commitment to Sartrean phenomenology, they have to concede that transcendence, as a sub-routine within a socially-conditioned consciousness, might, in reality, just be shoring up whatever would have needed transcending to begin with. Their current exit strategy, i.e., from out of this double-bind, is to claim that there must be two styles of transcendence. There's an ordinary transcendence that stays "immanent" within subjectivity, but there's also an extraordinary transcendence that irrupts into rhetorical transaction from nowhere.

So here's a statement from Grøn and Overgaard (2007) to contextualize the manner in which philosophers today can try to rescue transcendence from the very clutches of immanence:

> One prominent trend has been to conceive of…the movement of transcendence as being constitutive of subjectivity…Recently, the seemingly opposite point has been made: subjectivity is to be understood from

the transcendence of the other that breaks subjectivity open. (4)

Of course, transcendence as "constitutive of subjectivity" refers to the humble factory-work that normally goes on inside human interiority, with immanence as subjectivity's default condition. But that's hardly enough in a world where rhetoric's will to matter has turned into the will to make transcendence matter. Here, the transcendence that breaks subjectivity open must be conceptualized as coming from *outside* of immanence, the problem becoming that of wishing such an "outside" into existence.

So far as concerns rhetorical theory, the synergy between those two philosophical trends is most clearly instantiated in Calvin Schrag's *The Self after Postmodernity* (1997), where communicative interaction is said to be informed sometimes by an ordinary, constitutive, Sartrean transcendence, and sometimes by an extraordinary, irrecuperable, Lévinasian transcendence. In the writing of Lévinas, to be sure, the opposition is between "rhetoric," which is by nature oppressive, and conversation, which is inexplicably receptive (70). Obviously, the *rhetorical* theorists can't settle for exactly that, not even when they've found it "prudent" to side with Lévinas, the philosopher who has so fully addressed the relation between speech and transcendence (Schrag 100, 114, 137–8). Yet it's the same libretto (enlivened differentially by the fancy footwork) in Schrag, Hyde, and Turnbull as in Lévinas. Always, there's a miraculous intervention keeping rhetoricity transcendent despite itself. It's this unmotivated intercession from beyond, meriting the label of fideism, which we should hold not simply to characterize, but indeed to vitiate the existential-transversal account of rhetorical agency.

To begin with, writers like Schrag, Hyde, and Turnbull would readily accept that there can be a (limited) sort of transcendence *within* immanence, for their basic position can be formulated casuistically enough: "Radical transcendence operates transversally, and...the grammar of transversality replaces that of universality" (Schrag 130). Yet there's still the task of protecting the whole mechanism (grammar, transversality, and all) from those who could show it to be socially determined in the first place. And it's on this count that Schrag in particular sounds intractable: we can hardly expect genuine, authentic, radical transcendence to arise from "internal" or immanent critique, which latter would of course recirculate the immediately-given constraints upon subjectivity (126–129). Instead, the only critique adequate to the self after postmodernity will be "external," calling for a certain leap of faith.

The Fideistic Appeal

So let's consider the allure which Lévinasian phenomenology must hold for a thinker like Schrag. We'll turn to an argument quite central for Lévinas:

> When I perceive objects, I am their condition of manifestation, and they consequently appear as my creations. In contrast, my encounter with the Other is not conditioned by anything in my power, but can only offer itself from without, as an epiphanic visitation. (Zahavi 144)

That's to inaugurate the recent trend of splitting transcendence into two different styles. There's an ordinary, workaday transcendence, as is to be found in most other phenomenology, and yet there is, in addition, an extraordinary, radical transcendence, the "absolute experience" of which "is not disclosure but revelation" (Lévinas, qtd. in Zahavi 144).

Similarly, though not by coincidence, Schrag is also having to split transcendence into two. One of its styles, the Sartrean, is forever to risk recuperation into social logic. And the other, the Lévinasian, is forever to be protected by fideism. That's how Schrag can help rescue communication from immanence-in-disguise, that is, from the workaday kind of transcendence constructed by Husserl and Sartre, and then presupposed by writers like Jurgen Habermas.

Henceforth, communication will be animated by that excessive, uncontainable kind of transcendence so often registered, no matter how dimly, in the *religious*. And then the self (or agent) after postmodernity can be conceptualized in terms of that openness to radical alterity presented as theology in Augustine, but reclaimed for philosophy in Kierkegaard and Lévinas.

Schrag's task, therefore, is to establish a fideistic, Lévinasian exit from immanence-in-disguise. And here's a passage in which he begins doing so, declaring that what's

> no longer at issue is a transcendence-within-immanence, a transcendence within the economies of the human subject understanding itself in its discourse, action, perception, and communal involvements, but rather transcendence…understood as residing on the other side of the economies of human experience. (114)

Isn't it paradoxical to maintain that our merely human interactions can be animated by some power residing on the other side of everything? Well, if that's paradoxical, says the existential-transversal theorist, then so be it: the "grammar of faith is the grammar of paradox" (120). In that case, however, communication must be more or less synonymous with grace. For a transcendence so paradoxical as *that* (flouting our own "configurations of experience," our own "forms of life") would have nothing to do with us at all (Schrag 138–139).

The real mystery, however, is as to why the existential-transversal perspective on agency, with its concern for life, responsibility, conscience, questioning, and the rest, would be appealing to the grammar of paradox rather than to the structure of human embodiment. Thus we, as assemblage-theoretical investigators, find ourselves in the position of having to reinforce a certain stance on agency by recorporealizing it, and all on behalf of some of the local theorists themselves. Yet there's no reason, not even in this case, to posit any miracle: we can instead deploy an additional affordance of the existential-transversal perspective as such.

Correcting Forgetfulness through a Material Phenomenology

As it turns out, the other existential-transversal writers do have an ally who could help protect transcendence from social determination. It's the phenomenologist Michel Henry, whose outlier status may well be due to his recalcitrant treatment of transcendence as *immanent*. Yet Henry introduces an understanding of embodiment which (while correcting the generally idealist forgetfulness of materiality) ought to allow the other local theorists to see that rhetorical transaction really doesn't need to access any extrinsic, faith-based resources in order to effect genuine social change.

In his translator's introduction to *Material Phenomenology* (1990/2008), Scott Davidson portrays the late Michel Henry as articulating a "nonbiological concept" of "life" as a "transcendental auto-affectivity" (ix). Here, it's the pioneering work of Husserl (and, by implication, of Sartre) that becomes the target of critique: "There are many problems with Husserl's account of intersubjectivity, but for Henry all of these problems can… be traced to Husserl's decision to promote transcendence over the immanence of life" (Henry, *Material*, xiii). The analysis thus identifies the fatal limitation for not just Husserlian, but very much of post-Kantian thinking, a tradition in which even something so central as materiality has to be hypothesized rather than experienced.

In marked contrast to Schrag, Hyde, or Turnbull, Henry maintains that transcendent responsibility is grounded in human embodiment, preceding intersubjectivity and persisting within it. Indeed, the "intersubjective community…is joined together not through a shared perception of the world…but through the *pathos* of life" (Henry, *Material*, xiii). For, according to Henry, "there exists a more fundamental mode of being, immanence, which is the origin of all transcendence whatsoever" (xi). And this philosopher offers an uncompromisingly *gapless* account of immanence, where "an affection of life by life" becomes the "condition for any actual existence" (Williams, "Critical Contrasts," 266). In this view, "affect B" isn't transcendentally "caused by external cause A, or determined by condition A." For example, it's not that empathy is transcendentally constructed by consciousness. Instead, life inheres or insists in the affects of life, such that "affect B" is "determined by affect B."

As for the question of responsibility, Henry's answer will, as always, be that it's animated by pathos. This pure affectivity, primitive and invisible as we might take it to be, is accessible to us all, linking us *regardless* of our sociality. Indeed, much of Henry's "political and ethical work" is to "re-establish the primordial status of life as auto-affection," to "revalue affects — suffering, alienation, bewilderment — in political debate," and to contest the wrongful as "carried by the distinctions, goals and implications of the turn away from life" (Williams, "Critical Contrasts," 274).

We might then say that Henry is holding forth the clearest promise for de-subjectivizing rhetorical agency. In respecifying transcendence as immanent *before* consciousness (though, by implication, still operating transversally — in the auto-affectivity linking all of the existential selves) he neither ties it to any "historical idea," nor invites it into the world by fiat, but rather, refers it to human corporeality (Beauvoir, qtd. in Gothlin 54).

Borrowing now from Michel Henry's *Philosophy and Phenomenology of the Body* (1965/1975), we can do our part to restore the corporeality that's otherwise missing from the existential-transversal perspective. Because Henry's argument may be misconstrued if quoted too aphoristically, we'll view one of the relevant passages at length:

> Man is not essentially an historical being. He is always the same. Since it is here a question of the body...it will be objected that the human body presents...characteristics which have varied throughout the course of history...However, this is not the original body, but various ways in which man represents this body to himself and behaves toward it. What is historical are the cultural or human objects and the different human attitudes related thereto. But the ontological basis which founds both objects and attitudes is indif-

ferent to this evolution; the latter always presupposes
the ontological foundation. (4)

Thus Michel Henry really is advancing a philosophy for the living human being, not for the cerebrating subject of the social, or the transcendental jackalope, or some similarly neo-Kantian construct. Whereas other contemporary thinkers assume that consciousness must be the (grounding) determination of materiality in re-presentation, Henry views consciousness as the (figural) continuation of materiality by other means.

At this point, having worked hard enough at it, we can say we're in a place where rhetoricity, if it ever *does* conduce to the life-affirming (even for no necessary reason), must be accessing an agency that's intrinsic to the human being to begin with. This is an agency which arises not from conventionality or sociality or identity, but instead from a claim upon existence which inheres, irreducibly so, in everyone's embodiment. After all, in this particular landscape, if nowhere else, the agent's imperative is to *ek-sist*, which means to "stand out" against absence.
Lewis R. Gordon (2006) makes that point quite clearly. He argues that, for persons of color, what precedes even the problem of representation (including in the political sense) is the task of emerging beyond "indistinction"—of coming to stand out as present, visible, participating in the world (20). Yet Gordon also emphasizes that this is the task not just for certain, specially-designated social groups, but for everyone. It's our sharing in ek-sistence (and, let's add, in the original body, this latter's condition of possibility) that's actually connecting us all.

So, yes, as Schrag or Hyde or Turnbull ought to agree, this is the sort of sharing that unifies us by way of a transversal linkage, passing through any number of social or cultural or historical compartments. But transcendence now begins with auto-affection. It's authorized by the original body, and it's manifested (as Guattari would say) in these "instinctual demands" that travel everywhere, right along with the existential selves who transport them.

Rhetorical Agency and the Existential Self

Let's rejoin the now-recorporealized company of Sojourner Truth, who has carried her speech (the claim "I am a woman's rights," plus the package made up of *race, gender, work, mind, biblical precept,* and *embodiment,* as well as the metaphor of the pint and the quart) all the way into the existential-transversal landscape of agency. Clearly, in a place like this, there's nothing pivotal about the "I" of "I am a woman's rights," for the human claim to exist is already universal. Meanwhile, the "woman's" can hardly be central, since it's never the original body, but only the latter's secondary determinations that will have any gender. As for the "rights," they, too, must refer to something peripheral, to those collectively-held values that keep coming and going with every shift in the social. This time, therefore, it'll be the "am" which is salient. In that case, let's start asking how communication about an "am" could ever, even as far back as 1851, afford an opportunity for certain existential and ethical imperatives to come into contact, to begin interacting synergistically, and then to give rise to just the sort of rhetorical agency that would conduce to genuine social change.

For an approach to an answer, let's consider that, from the existential-transversal perspective, Sojourner Truth's famous speech must be designed to connect certain forms of social identity (or of essence) by demonstrating these always already to be linked at the level of the original body (or of existence). We do know, from the work of Michel Henry, something about that original body, and now we need to find out something about those forms of social identity. If we turn to the work of the historian Nell Irvin Painter, we'll soon see that, in this case, the two most relevant social identities are those of *feminist* and *abolitionist.*

In the following passage, Painter is explaining the historical significance of Sojourner Truth's message, her statement. She writes,

> One of only a few black women regulars on the feminist and antislavery circuit, Truth...was the pivot that linked two causes — of women (presumed to be

white) and of blacks (presumed to be men) — through one black female body. (*Sojourner Truth*, 171)

Upon reflection, we realize that the passage is already demythologizing the presumption that Sojourner Truth's rhetorical agency could derive from her social identity as a woman, or even as a black woman. So far as concerned the mid-nineteenth century status quo, someone who wasn't white couldn't be a woman, anyway, not in the public forum. Perhaps such a figure might be a female, or maybe a quasi-woman, but not much more than that. Besides, as Painter does explain in detail, not even the feminists of the day could have arrived at any consensus on black women's social identity. Some of the most important such activists were then advocating gender-egalitarianism exclusively *within* the familiar constraints of race and class. In recognizing the interests of white women only, these (non-abolitionist) feminists would effectively frame all others as non-women. So it's not that Sojourner Truth could just show up at some feminist convention of 1851 and already be, for example, a woman.

Meanwhile, in the speech that we're studying, the speaker is front-stage and center, submitted to all sorts of scrutiny — and not by just anyone, but specifically by those seeking to work out the rights of gender. Could her self-disclosures then be for the patriarchs (so very few of whom would be attending, or even attending to, any woman's rights convention of 1851)? Of course not: her speech must, instead, be for the undecided among the feminists, those still wondering whether it'd be an error to allow an *abolitionist* like Sojourner Truth (threatening, by association, to bring along with her the "blacks" who are "presumed to be men") into the women's movement at all (Painter, *Sojourner Truth*, 171).

Under such circumstances, even the gender of the speaker's voice becomes an issue. After all, the historical Sojourner Truth is known for speaking in a voice so "robust" and "deep" that "that some of her enemies" have "suspected" she's "a man" (Campbell 12). But, in that case, we're left with a figure even *less* categorizable as a woman than before. It's perplexing enough that being black disqualifies the speaker from any self-evident status as a woman. And now there's the very timbre of her voice to take into consideration.

So we've arrived at a puzzle. It's unclear how Sojourner Truth, this difficult quantity, could possibly accomplish what the historian Nell Irving Painter would claim, that is, by becoming the "pivot" that links the "feminist" cause with the "antislavery" cause (*Sojourner Truth* 171). And that's to say nothing of what the rhetorical theorist Karlyn Kohrs Campbell would claim, i.e., with respect to the speaker's stepping up to lead a monolithically black-and-feminist onslaught against the patriarchy.

To be sure, a commentator like Schrag, or Hyde, or Turnbull might wish to respond that the speaker is benefiting from her ineffable Otherness, which must be introducing some radical (consciousness-raising) transcendence into the mix. Nevertheless, the more tenable existential-transversal answer would be that our exemplary rhetorical agent must, in the very process of speaking to the question of equal rights, have annihilated the presumption that social identity could matter in the first place.

On Pivoting, Transcendence, and Emergence

Indeed, if we retain from the Frances Dana Gage account of the speech whatever is corroborated in the Marius Robinson account, we find that the Sojourner Truth who speaks in 1851 is, in some respects, outside all of the then-salient social categories, and yet, in some other respects, inside all of them, too. Thus it becomes evident that she must be dramatizing, in her own person, the capacity of the existential self not only to exceed any of the contemporary essences, but also to pass through them (transversally) along the way.

To begin with, the speaker describes a seeming state of diremption among the salient socio-political groups, with the implication that any genuine change would require some reconciliation among those alienated parties. In the process, however, she also reveals herself to be *exempt* from that sort of partisanship, and all on account of her not belonging (at least not intrinsically so) to any of the factions in question. Indeed, in portraying division or alienation as a secondary condition, as an effect or outcome of social relations, she's suggesting that there might very well exist a form of connection or consubstantiality that's prior to any collective determination whatever.

According to the Robinson version of the speech, which historians and biographers do consider quite reliable, Sojourner Truth observes that "the women are coming up blessed by God and a few of the men are coming up with them. But man is in a tight place, the poor slave is on him, woman is coming on him, and he is surely between a hawk and a buzzard" (Painter, *Sojourner Truth*, 126). Meanwhile, according to the less reliable Gage, what the speaker says is this: "Well, chilern, whar dar is so much racket dar must be somethin' out o' kilter. I tink dat 'twixt de niggers of de Souf and de womin at de Norf, all talkin' 'bout rights, de white men will be in a fix pretty soon" (Campbell 9). So where's the state of socio-political diremption that we're seeking? Well, it's disclosed in the separation of the terms "man," "woman," and "slave."

On the one side, there might perhaps be "man" and, on the other side, there might perhaps be "woman" and "slave" (folded into a sort of phalanx). Even so, while we can see that "man" and "slave" form one clear-cut binary, just as "man" and "woman" form another, we cannot see any clear-cut relation between "slave" and "woman." The hawk is a different entity from the buzzard, and, yes, each of the two may be mounting its own assault. But it's not that "man" is having to contend with a hawk-buzzard, or with an alliance between buzzard and hawk.

Indeed, the men, the slaves, and the women are described as occupying separate compartments within the social. The distance is geographical as well as ideational; it's literal, physical, regional, and not only cultural and political. The men are everywhere, so there's no need for the speaker to specify their location. But "de niggers," come to think of it, would be quite definitively in "de Souf." And "de womin" — the feminists — would be quite definitively "at de Norf." At this moment, then, it's diremption wherever we turn. It's alienation betwixt the (white) men and the (white) Northern feminists, and it's alienation between the (black) Southern slaves and the (white) men, and it's also, though independently, alienation among the (white) Northern feminists, the (black) Southern slaves, and, of course, the (white) men, too.

Nevertheless, as we reflect on the state of separation depicted in both the Gage and Robinson versions of the speech, we realize that the speaker has presented herself as *missing* from all of the social classifications at issue. While the white men, the black slaves, and the white women each belong to some prepared-for place, the speaker doesn't. After all, the place of the white men is everywhere, unlike the place of Sojourner Truth. Yet this speaker is not a slave, for she has famously been "freed by New York law" some twenty-five years earlier (Campbell 8). Furthermore, she can't be one of "de niggers of de Souf," since she isn't even where they are. To the contrary, she's up North, and among the "regulars on the feminist and antislavery circuit" (Painter, *Sojourner Truth*, 171). But, then again, the North is the place of "de womin," and the jury's currently out as to whether the speaker fits into that category.

We must conclude that nobody, at the present moment, can say whether Sojourner Truth is a slave or not a slave, a woman or not a woman, or even, for that matter, a man or not a man, what with her voice so "robust" and so "deep" (Mabee and Newhouse, qtd. in Campbell 12). That's what it must mean for someone, *circa* 1851, to be constituting a liminal site. But regardless that it's impossible to assign Sojourner Truth to any of the contemporary categories, here she is, anyway. And if she's still affirming the possibility of some consubstantiality or connection with her auditors, then she must be declaring that everyone here can be conjoined in a manner somehow independent of any collectively-determined identity.

That's quite as we should expect in a world like the one we're visiting now. For the whole point of theorizing rhetorical transaction from within the existential-transversal frame is to construct speech as accessing transcendence (and in an transversal manner, at that). In this instance, what needs to be overcome is, on the one side, the category of gender and, on the other side, the category of race, and Sojourner Truth is overcoming these by not belonging to either.

But that's only because our exemplary rhetorical agent, if she's ever to become a pivot between the feminist movement and the abolitionist movement, has initially to speak as a person, and only later on as a woman and/or an African-American. To do that requires her to clear away any presumptions, on the one side, as to her gender identity and, on the other side, as to her racial identity, leaving in the middle (front-stage and center) only her ontologically prior claim to exist as a human being. That's how she's to dramatize that just any other existential self, whether currently essentialized as a woman, or an African-American, or something else, can also precede, occupy, and transcend its given social positioning. Indeed, while it's clear from both Robinson and Gage that the speaker does testify from personal experience, we are still to discover, if we triangulate carefully enough, that the autobiographical references have nothing to do either with black or with being female.

To begin with, if we rule out of consideration all those emblems of femininity that are (a) so routinely sutured to Sojourner Truth's statement (the mother's grief, the thirteen children, the part about not being "helped into carriages") and yet (b) so conspicuously absent from the Robinson version, appearing only in the fictionalized, melodramatic version from Gage, we find that the speaker's claim, her advocating on behalf of the disenfranchised, cannot turn on her status as a woman.

According to Robinson himself, the speaker never includes any verification as to her gender identity at all. True, her strategy is to keep emphasizing that she's not a man, so that she consistently proceeds by negation:

> I have as much muscle as any man, and can do as much work as any man. I have plowed and reaped and husked and chopped and mowed, and can any man do more than that?...I can carry as much as any man, and can eat as much too...I am as strong as any man that is now. (Painter, *Sojourner Truth*, 125)

But if we isolate the key terms — muscle, work, plowed, reaped, husked, chopped, mowed, carry, eat, strong — we realize, as would so many a woman of the nineteenth century, that they have only to do with being an embodied person authenticating her claim to existence.

So, having dismissed the possibility that Sojourner Truth's gender might be speaking before she does, we'll inquire into the possibility that her race might be exerting priority over her humanity. We do notice some markers of race in the Gage version of the speech, saturated as it is with dialect. But there's no time like the present to recall that the dialect is bogus:

> Truth did not speak in the language that Gage attributed to her; even her most powerful arguments and apt metaphors were by this language deformed, even ridiculed. Note, too, that this is the only extant text or fragment in which Truth uses the n-word. (Campbell 13)

Consequently, if we, as investigators of the Gage account, agree to discount the fabricated dialect, we really can't hear any blackness at all.

Meanwhile, Robinson's account contains exactly no linguistic traces as to the speaker's racial identity. His Sojourner Truth doesn't sound even slightly black, not by any criterion of 1851. Instead, she sounds like anybody else, for she's speaking the "standard English" which, as Campbell divulges, so often characterized her public communication (Campbell 12).

More intriguing yet, if there's any hint in Robinson as to Sojourner Truth's racial identity, it's — at most — that the speaker is an "emancipated slave," which still doesn't tell us anything much. Here, we can refer to the work of Frederick Douglass, Sojourner Truth's colleague on some of the same speaking tours. In Chapter 7 of his *Narrative* (1845), Douglass recalls helping the Irish laborers with their work on the docks. He's asked whether he's "a slave for life," and this is for him to discover the reality of indenture. That's a practice in which almost anyone of less-than-modest means — say, an Irishman — might end up as a *temporary* slave, though perhaps for years at a time. So, for Marius Robinson to report on the speaker as an "emancipated slave" isn't, after all, for him to label her by race.

By now, we must rule out any linguistic markers that would define the speaker either as female or as black. So we can no longer maintain that her rhetorical agency would emanate from some social identity leaking through her words. But, in that case, if we're eliminating or suspending so much of the language of the speech, then what's left for us to talk about? Well, it's not as if we're abandoning everything that's linguistic about the speech. We're simply noting that, if Sojourner Truth is speaking without foregrounding either her race or her gender, then she can't be speaking like an identity politician. It's an existential, rather than ideological content that she's communicating.

At this stage, our exemplary rhetorical agent has disclosed herself as a person, as standing, so to speak, prior to the social categories of "woman" and "black." From this point on, she can almost effortlessly shift into either or both of those social categories, but while remaining herself in the process. And when she does shift into this or that familiar identity, what will be already be there, populating the categories of the day? The answer is that an array of other existential selves will already be there. These will be all of the persons, whether in the immediate audience or elsewhere, who are as capable as Sojourner Truth of stepping into all sorts of social identities, but without thereby doffing their personhood. So, collectively, the speaker and the audience will constitute the entire populace of the existential-transversal world, and then Sojourner Truth will speak for everybody in the same breath as she speaks for herself.

In sum, if Sojourner Truth really is a rhetorical agent, her auditors (existential selves, every last one of them) will recognize that "the signs to be interpreted" in her message, "however connected to still other signs," are "nevertheless trying to convey something true" (Grondin 58). They will grasp her statement as an "event of speaking" in which "someone" is "saying something to someone" (Schrag 22). While the someone who does the saying will not be interchangeable with the someone who does the listening, and while the selves engaged in the transaction will, in any case, be "emergent" rather than fixed, each of the participants will nevertheless be an "I," a somebody (Schrag 22, 26). And all of them will be linked through something prior to, and independent of, any socially-determined identity, something inherent in an irreducible (because emergent) "am." It's the human claim to exist, a claim which, even as it differentiates every speaking self, also hybridizes every "I" with the self of its other.

The Rhetorical Agent and the Original Body

Yet the question remains as to the mechanism(s) through which an exemplary rhetorical practitioner—having, as it were, preempted her own reduction to race or gender—could affirm the link between herself and her interlocutors. Surely the answer will have to concern human corporeality, which is, as Michel Henry would say, auto-affectively included within any social identity to which a listener may belong. Yet we shouldn't jump to conclusions as to what the audience members would witness in fixing their disparate gazes upon the speaker.

For, when we ourselves scrutinize the intersection between our two sources, Robinson and Gage, all that comes into view is what Michel Henry calls the *original body*, which isn't a matter of the speaker's race or gender, or even of the merely verbal signs through which she's announcing her existence. Indeed, while Gage and Robinson together assure us that the original body is quite actively involved in this transaction, they also confirm, each of them in a different way, that it cannot disappear into symbolization.

As Karlyn Kohrs Campbell points out, Gage does dwell on Sojourner Truth's conversion of physicality into a non-verbal rhetorical device. So here's the passage from Gage, including that reporter's authorial intrusion: "'Look at me! Look at my arm!'...and she bared her right arm to the shoulder, showing her tremendous muscular power" (Campbell 10). Nell Irvin Painter analyzes the scenario as follows:

> Gage shines a spotlight on Truth's body: a massive, towering figure straining upward...undressed and on display...Gage describes Truth's disrobing a part of her body. The naked limb is a mighty right arm,

the arm of a worker, the arm of a powerful woman. (*Sojourner Truth* 171)

According to Gage, at least, Sojourner Truth doesn't vanish into some epistemic wrinkle, or into the recesses of the sign. We know it because Sojourner Truth is *bypassing* representation, baring her non-linguistic arm, and during no less than the process of affirming her existential claim.

Now, if we have read from Annemarie Mol (2002), we might remember that even arteries can acquire a gender, maybe a race as well, and we might concede that Sojourner Truth's arm could quite possibly, at some ontically subsequent moment, take on just those determinations. We might further appreciate that Sojourner Truth's arm does seem distinguished from that of someone who'd never lifted a finger. But how can this be the arm of a woman, or of a black woman, or of a black woman who's a worker, before it's the arm of a person?

It's as a person, then — not as a social identity — that Sojourner Truth is speaking, and it's the original body that's manifested in her speech. Not everyone in the audience will be a black woman used to performing manual labor, or inclined to identify with the speaker on that basis. Yet everyone will have a share in the original body, whether instantiated by an arm, a face, or something else. If it's an arm, though, the arm will be enough like Sojourner Truth's for everyone to have something in common. Proprioception alone (returning us to Guattari's conception of the "instinctual" demand) will mean that the speaker's incarnation can't be dismissed as theatricality, written off as signification, for this is now a body just as real as mine.

Yet Sojourner Truth's original body precedes any particularly "social" attributes (any blackness, femaleness, whiteness, maleness, workerliness), just as it precedes any of the verbal signs wrapped around it. Therefore, if Gage is affirming that Sojourner Truth bares her arm as part of the performance, then Gage is affirming that there's a layer to rhetorical agency which, though palpable, cannot be represented. Not even Gage can do more than gesture towards it, and only in an indication that redoubles, rather than interprets, the exemplary speaker's gesture: Here's this material existence which we're, all of us, sharing.

And then, if we do continue triangulating, we'll discover that an unrepresentable embodiment is participating in the Robinson version of the speech as well. For, just as soon as we allow that account back into the archive, we discover some additional evidence that the original body, the one which Sojourner Truth is manifesting in her speech, cannot be black, or female, or both. Robinson verifies, even more clearly than does Gage, that Sojourner Truth becomes a rhetorical agent by virtue not of her social visibility but of her irreducible embodiment. So here is the preface to his version of Sojourner Truth's statement:

> One of the most unique and interesting speeches of the Convention was made by Sojourner Truth, an emancipated slave. It is impossible to transfer it to paper, or convey any adequate idea of the effect it produced upon the audience. Those only can appreciate it who saw her powerful form, her whole-souled, earnest gestures, and listened to her strong and truthful tones. (Painter, *Sojourner Truth*, 125)

And, in that case, we need to ask what's happened to Sojourner Truth's blackness and/or femaleness now.

As we've found earlier, the speaker's racial and gender identity aren't anywhere in the speech as Robinson presents it. But they're not even in the editorial *preface* to the speech, considering that "emancipated slave" could, in the middle of the nineteenth century, refer to an Irishman. As for the speaker's gender, well, the only traces are metadiscursive. They belong to the reporter's "her" and "she," which don't in the least impinge upon the argument. In short, all we are being given to understand in Robinson's introduction is that you'd just have to share in the original body — in that unrepresentable "form" which exists before any socially-recuperable content — to grasp what's happening in the transaction. It's the form of any person who is armed, so to speak, with some human corporeality. So it's the original body, auto-affectively shared by everyone, that emerges out of indistinction in Robinson's account.

From this perspective, what goes for *race* and *gender* goes for "mind" as well, explaining the functionality of the pint-and-quart analogy. In both the Gage and Robinson versions of the speech, the speaker is portrayed as satirically engaging the question as to whether women and African-Americans should qualify for equal rights on the basis of their intelligence. But any bona fide argument along those lines would overlook that one's fundamental claim is already self-validating. So, on the existential-transversal view, the metaphor of the pint and the quart would be to *eradicate* the preoccupation with "intellect," leaving the audience in direct contact with the original body, for whom "mind" or "intelligence" is peripheral, anyway.

In short, the rhetorical agent to whom we can attribute this famous speech isn't essentially black, or female, or both. To the contrary, she's essentially human, mobile, and emergent. She's as human, mobile, and emergent as her interlocutors, all of whom, sharing the original body of the existential self, are able, just like her, not only to take on but also to transcend any socially-given identities.

A Re-Corporealized Transversality

By now, the Sojourner Truth speech is less about patriarchy, pure and simple, than about the relation (or not) between race and gender. Yet we still need to find out how this speaker could ever emerge as a "pivot" between the "antislavery" movement, populated primarily by men, and the "feminist" movement, populated primarily by women (Painter, *Sojourner Truth*, 171). This practitioner couldn't very well be a pivot beforehand, having, as it were, no self-evident leverage in either social camp to begin with, not at a time when "women" are "presumed to be white," and "blacks" are "presumed to be men." So she must be converting herself into a pivot during the rhetorical transaction itself.

Let's examine the process through which Sojourner Truth manages to express her own personhood in just such a manner as (transversally) to link the socially recognizable figure of the black person with the socially recognizable figure of the woman. Certainly, it's in order to effect such a connection that the speaker is working "race" and "gender" into the speech to begin with. As it turns out, the avenue for transcendence opens up not at either of those sites, but, rather (and once again) at the site of *biblical precept*. We know it because both Robinson and Gage portray the speaker as continually referencing Jesus.

It's true that Christ is associated with the very religion which happens, *circa* 1851, to be the most prevalent within the social dispensation. But, in addition to that, and separately from that, Jesus is emblematic of the existential self, which is why you don't have to be black and/or female to respond to Him. For Jesus acts as an existential-transversal collector, and as an existential-transversal separator, too. He gathers what's prior about the existential self, distantiating all of that from what's secondary about sociality. By the same token, Jesus bespeaks, at one and the same time, such definitively existential-transversal preoccupations as finitude or lack, the original body, ek-sistence, revolution, emancipation, the absolute if counter-rational rejection of arbitrary constraint, and, above all, the reality of transcendence.

In that case, "biblical precept" functions primarily as a vehicle for bringing Jesus into the conversation. And then Jesus (sharing the original body, too) becomes a middle term, a mediator, translating the speaker into existential commensurability with her auditors — black, white, feminist, abolitionist, whatever. This is how Sojourner Truth demonstrates, in person, that anybody can be an advocate simultaneously for women's rights and for African-Americans' rights. After all, if she is concerned for African-Americans and women, then she (like Jesus, and like the followers of Jesus) must existentially be not only an African-American but also a woman, emerging as such because of her concern for anyone.

What is, shall we say, crucial about the interchange is that it *redistribute*s the speaker's care, quite in keeping with the thesis which Elaine Scarry (1985), evidently another of these existential-transversal thinkers, advances with regard to the workings of mediation more generally. But it's Sojourner Truth's own claim to exist, and to share in the personhood of her auditors (who, again, might accidentally be positioned within just any social classification), that familiarizes everybody with the new, blended category of the "black female." It's a category, after all, which any other existential self may enter or exit as readily as she can. That, finally is how the speaker becomes a "pivot" between the initially-alienated constituencies. For she's at least doubled the set of agents who, in their consubstantiality both with black people (plus abolitionists) and with women (plus feminists), are prepared to accept this transversal advocacy for extending equal rights to everyone.

6.
Materiality in the Material-Semiotic Landscape

RESEARCHERS FROM ANY WORKSPACE other than the existential-transversal ought to be left perplexed at the idea that rhetorical transcendence could be scaffolded upon so little as an original (human) body accompanied by an (authentic) existential claim. But we'll move on to the fourth landscape of rhetorical agency. It's the material-semiotic perspective, where rhetoric's will to matter has become the will to make materiality matter. Here, the practitioner involved in rhetorical transaction won't necessarily possess either an original body or an existential claim. Instead, this will be an actor that can take on all sorts of properties and/or functionalities, depending on the specific assemblages in which he, she, it, they, or we might be implicated. So the rhetorical agent in question must be an *ineffable participant*: a term whose concrete, though not necessarily physical materiality forever exceeds the semiotic relations by which it's contextualized.

A Parable of Materiality-and-Relationality

The terms "material" and "semiotic" may sound ubiquitous, but relatively few commentators within rhetorical studies have adopted any material-semiotic approach as such. The label, as we'll employ it, comes from the actor-network theorist John Law (2009). While the "material" part does, roughly speaking, refer to objects, tools, things, corporealities, the "semiotic" part refers to relationships. In this context, "semiotics is not limited to signs," for it's "the study of order building or path building and may be applied to settings, machines, bodies, and programming languages as well as texts" (Akrich and Latour 259). Unfortunately, so far as concerns the study of rhetorical agency, the genuinely material-semiotic treatments can be difficult to recognize, especially if they eschew labels like "material-semiotic." But a good example — worth keeping in mind as a parable — is Carmen Werder's "Rhetorical Agency: Seeing the Ethics of It All" (2000).

Werder discovers that agency (here known as "persuasion") ripples across networks which are themselves under construction — that is, by all sorts of "rhetorical" agents, rather than by human actors alone. In her case study, agency turns out to be an internally-variegated alliance, where intentionality, influence, authority, disparate social roles, technological affordances, persons, and power, including of the "physical" kind, are assembled in such a manner as to produce some genuine social change (Werder 20).

As the story goes, Werder is tasked with administering a certain writing proficiency examination, the latter proving to be quite a "bad test" (15). In urging the adoption of a better form of assessment, she struggles to exert some power, authority, and influence, getting nowhere in the process. But then she becomes a consultant to a committee, joins a task force, visits thirty-two departments, meets with follow-up focus groups. Over time, she finds herself hooked up within a network reaching so far that the important decision makers get folded into it too. Meanwhile, among the participants, there's an "economics professor" who almost coincidentally drafts a successful recommendation "for replacing the exam" (17). Yes, it's been a matter of putting "people in conversation," and of working "sophistically," as by "analyzing the situation and taking advantage of... kairotic moments." On the other hand, as we should also note, the kairos and conversationality have themselves joined forces with some non-trivial materialities (witness the badness of the test that really has "to go"), and with some shared values, and even with some free choice (16).

Now, the replacement of the undesirable state of affairs by something better is evidence of social change, and Werder has played an indispensable role. Yet it's not Werder but her cyborg that has done the persuading — which isn't to imply that the latter's co-constituents could all be cut from the same cloth. For example, since Werder (singled out, from among myriads, for inspection) is not an economist, and since the economics professor is not a writing program administrator, they cannot be identically interested. Even so, these disparate stakeholders have performed what the rhetorical theorist Clay Spinuzzi would call some "net work," some mutually-beneficial "translation," producing certain "composite goals differing from the existing ones," and together generating a new materiality (16, 88).

Assemblaging, Stratification, and Circulating Reference

Shadowing the trail followed by agents like Werder, we'll start investigating the production of rhetorical materiality — particularly of the kind that materializes transcendence. We'll soon team up with Sojourner Truth, who, in turn, will be connecting certain disparate collectivities, such that rhetorical agency (some of it hers) begins to ripple from one end of the alliance to the other. But, before that, there are two more assemblage-theoretical constructs for us to internalize, and these involve *stratification* and *circulating reference*.

Let's recall that, for Deleuze, both "reterritorialization" and "deterritorialization" refer to social processes that may lead to coherence despite heterogeneity. A complementary, though still Deleuzean frame for thinking about the problem of coherence is to view it as "stratification," where territories, or strata, stand for "historical formations...made from things and words, from seeing and speaking, from the visible and the sayable, from bands of visibilities and fields of readability, from contents and expressions" (Deleuze and Guattari, *ATP*, 88). But "contents" aren't limited to meanings, ideas, and the like, for they include the materiality of social interchange, which latter becomes an "intermingling of bodies reacting to one another." Meanwhile, "expressions" aren't limited to linguistic utterances, for they bespeak the relationality of social interchange. Indeed, the sayable, readable "words" include not only "statements," but also "acts," which might very well be other than symbolistic.

So, here in the material-semiotic world, social interaction takes place within and between strata. Further, it involves terms (bodies, words, etc.) that are both irreducible to relations (structures, discursive formations, and the like) and separable from them. After all, "it is not impossible to make a radical break between regimes of signs and their objects" (Deleuze and Guattari, *ATP*, 7). As a result, social interaction often gives rise to entirely new realities, such as by effecting "incorporeal transformations attributed to bodies" (88). We can just look around to see that this is what's happened, for example, to Gandhi, mutating from (a) some provincial gadfly in South Africa, to (b) a bona fide figurehead for Indian national independence. It's in many ways the same Gandhi, yet the one undergoing the incorporeal transformation has become multiplied in the interaction among all sorts of "contents" and "expressions."

Having glanced at the import (and composition) of Deleuzean strata, we'll turn to the concept of circulating reference, which is a Latourian way of describing the material-and-semiotic communication taking place among radically disparate agents. Latour's (1999) illustrations concern the work of a small group of researchers, soil scientists who are studying the border between the forest and the savanna in an Amazonian province. The results will be circulated, passed along in ladder-like chains of reference, with ramifications reaching potentially everywhere. At any rate, some parts of the savanna become remediated as they mingle with scientific practices, with concepts, with bits and pieces of equipment. They give rise to moisture samples, botanical samples, other sorts of samples, entering into articulation with color codes, charts, photographs, numbers, words. But reference is occurring incrementally, and it's taking place in both directions.

As Timothy Webmoor (2007) explains, Latour's scientists "transubstantiate or translate a given piece of soil into a code on a Munsell soil chart." The result is that a segment of color-code "takes the place of the original situation" (Latour, *Pandora's*, 67). So we might already notice the affinity between Deleuzean stratification and Latourian circulating reference. There are terms in relation at every ladder-like point between the savanna and the finished article, but all of the terms are detachable from all of the relations.

Even so, Latour's insight is that it's not the fault of the savanna, or of the soil, or of the pedologist, or of the sample, or even of the code, if some reader skims the scientific article without scrutinizing the quite traceable linkages underlying its construction. After all, each locus of activity (for example, that tiny chunk of the continent in question) is now positioned to talk back to any agents who might wish, traveling down the ladder of reference, to interview it for themselves. Thus, on the Latourian account, circulating reference is communication which, coming or going, links those participants who are actually (not to say theoretically) interacting.

We can see that both Latourian circulating reference and Deleuzean stratification are operative even in the interaction studied by Carmen Werder (2000). There, communication is the interaction among staff, faculty, documents, values, policies, practices, perspectives, and many other participants, all of them becoming connected in a chain of incremental articulations, of interstitial mediations. Meanwhile, communication in Werder's case study is also a matter of the collaborative reality-building that can be performed by agents from all sorts of assemblages, territories, quasi-worlds. And, precisely because Werder is reporting on none other than rhetorical agency, rhetorical agency itself must be stratification, and circulating reference, too.

So, capitalizing on these ideas from Deleuze and Latour, let's agree that any participant acting within or between strata will not only belong to a chain of mediations, but also function as a circulating referent. Such a participant can as easily shore up certain local realities (as when a bit of color code contributes to a finished scientific article) as enunciate or transport certain local realities (as when the same bit of color code really does embody a piece of the savanna). Thus the work of the circulating referent is indeed the work of the material-semiotic rhetorical agent, whose imperative, again, is to make materiality matter.

In what follows, we'll start construing rhetorical materiality, the kind folded into rhetorical agency, as produced in the communicative interaction among participants who, though initially coming from different collectivities, gradually become implicated in the project of making things otherwise than they are. We'll treat our representative speaker, Sojourner Truth, as, in some respects, a resident within some quite separate strata *(biblical precept, race,* and *gender)* but, in some other respects, as an envoy, traveling among territories and connecting them. More specifically, we'll frame her as a circulating referent, creating linkages among her disparately-interested religious, abolitionist, and feminist constituencies, and helping establish an assemblage for materializing some genuine social change.

Entering at Biblical Precept

As we'll recall from the social-structural world, it's a "miracle" for even an exemplary rhetorical agent to be able to speak at all (Campbell 8). But we can now disaggregate the miracle, including by adopting a material-and-semiotic perspective on the steps through which a Sojourner Truth might be produced. Certainly, to report on everything would require that we leave most of it out. So that's what we'll do during the rest of our visit to the material-semiotic landscape of rhetorical agency.

If we wanted to go back to the beginning, we could describe our prospective rhetorical agent as *plasmatic* — as "not yet formatted, not yet measured, not yet socialized, not yet engaged in metrological chains, and not yet covered, surveyed, mobilized, or subjectified" (Latour, *Reassembling*, 244). But let's save time, picking up at a moment just before this anticipatory being (who, like any other term without a relation, is only in an ante-chamber to agency) has started belonging to any assemblages to speak of. How, then, can such a proto-speaker ever emerge into agency, ever acquire a relation of her own? The answer will, of course, have to do with stratification(s), and with circulating reference(s), and with incorporeal transformations(s).

As it turns out, our — shall we say — larval practitioner is transported all the way out of the antechamber, and all the way into a Christian assemblage of the earlier nineteenth century, two or three decades before she materializes at the famous women's rights convention of 1851. Initially, she's thrown amidst a family of Dutch-speaking African-Americans, enslaved, living in upstate New York. But the young Isabella, whose "earliest religious instruction" comes "from her mother," makes "a sanctuary on an island in the middle of a stream," where she goes "to talk with God and repeat the Lord's prayer" (Painter, "Difference," 143). In 1826, Jesus appears to her, and she experiences "a conversion." Her son Peter is "sold South," yet, with the aid of some Quakers and a pair of Dutch lawyers, she wins a court case for his return ("Difference" 143; see also Painter, *Sojourner Truth* 32–37). Around this time, she is "freed by New York law" (Campbell 8). She embraces Methodism, becoming friends with a teacher, the Methodist Miss Grear, and she helps found "the Kingston Methodist Church" (Painter, "Difference," 143; *Sojourner Truth* 27). So it's already the case that the mother, the religious instruction, the conversion experience, the conscientious Quakers, and the Methodists are constituting at least some of Isabella's rhetorical agency, since they're effectively formatting her for the stratum of *biblical precept*.

In 1828, our prospective rhetorical agent goes off to New York City with the Grears, who, like herself, are "Methodist perfectionists" (Painter, *Sojourner Truth,* 27). Yet her "religious sensibility" has become as "syncretic" as that of other "country people" in the region (25). It blends "beliefs and habits from animist West Africa and pagan Europe, the Calvinist Dutch Reformed Church and the Arminian Methodists," to which are "added the enthusiasms of the Second Great Awakening, when Methodist-style camp meetings" remediate many of the "Presbyterians and Congregationalists" as well. As we can see, the terrain is heterogeneous. Yet Isabella is hybridizing many of its local patches, as by belonging to them all.

By now, there is, in New York, a white Methodist church for Isabella to attend, and, after that, a Zion African church, established by black Methodists who have "experienced racial discrimination" at the other place of worship (Painter, "Difference," 143). Either way, Isabella has become folded into a Methodist assemblage, the latter's "dominant relation" taking the form of an intense interest in salvation (Baugh 36). In fact, Isabella herself starts preaching, Methodist-style, at "camp meetings," effecting "many conversions," and earning "great respect in various Methodist circles" (Painter, "Difference," 143). Clearly, she's no longer plasmatic. Instead, she's a circulating referent, and already shoring up the stratum of *biblical precept*.

Yet our exemplary speaker, though belonging to a majoritarian stretch of the terrain, belongs to some minoritarian stretches as well. For she's joined the Latourettes, a "dissident Methodist" couple whose own "disciples" are always "itinerant preachers," never fully "connected with any formal church" (Painter, "Difference," 144). And now we have an explanation as to Sojourner Truth's anomalousness among the "nineteenth black woman spiritualists," who did tend to "seek biblical authorization or acceptance from others regarding" their "ministry" (King, *Essence*, 137–39). It's not that she's a colossal individual too authentic to need allies. It's that her pathway has linked her with a collectivity actively supporting the work of the itinerant, dissident, even unauthorized preacher.

Then, through none other than these dissident if still Methodist Latourettes, our representative rhetorical agent is introduced into the "Christian" enough "commune" led by one emphatically apocalyptic Matthias (Painter, "Difference," 144–45). Isabella remains his "supporter" for a decade, until the "kingdom" founders, right around the time of a major economic recession. She's homeless. But, on the other hand, she's an experienced speaker, a competent preacher, and an apocalyptic Christian, all of it picked up through her interaction with other participants in the stratum of *biblical precept*. That's why, in 1843, when God speaks to her, "commanding her to quit the city and take a new name," Isabella can turn into "Sojourner Truth" (145–146). But what is the truth that this itinerant must be telling? Well, since she does take to the road in a year that is the very "apogee of Millerism" (a Christian movement apocalyptic enough to embrace her), we can be sure that it's a truth about the imminent destruction of everything.

So our exemplary rhetorical practitioner proves capable of speaking not only among the Methodists but among the millenarians, too. She's linked up with as material-semiotic an *agencement* as any actor-network (and/or media-ecological) theorist could envision. For the Millerite message, which creates tangible linkages among "hundreds of thousands of people," from "Maine to Michigan," is being spread through "a series of widely-distributed periodicals," as well as through "the teachings of scores of itinerant preachers" holding forth at "frequent and massive camp meetings" (Painter, "Difference,"146). And Sojourner Truth herself finds "a ready welcome" when she speaks at these gatherings "by the score" (146, 149).

To be sure, *biblical precept* must be a stratum where race and gender don't matter. Our evidence is that Sojourner Truth (whom some might categorize as an emancipated slave, a black person, a woman) not only meets no resistance, but actually receives a ready welcome. Perhaps that's because, back then, "Agency and independence gained through studying Christian doctrine," and "active participation in women's groups combined with their religious faith" did help so "many women to emancipate themselves from society's oppressive gender conventions" (King 120). And, yes, it does seem that, for Sojourner Truth at this juncture, there's some of almost everything: religious faith, doctrine, active participation, independence, and agency.

But where are the "women's groups"? The answer is that they're someplace else, located within another cyborg entirely. Indeed, this present assemblage is actively excluding the essentially political, and Sojourner Truth is caught up in the work of exclusion. For she's concentrating exclusively on materializing salvation. She's helping both to de-realize gender and to un-produce race, all of it in the interest of shoring up *biblical precept*.

We'll pursue the point by examining Sojourner Truth's current audiences more closely. These include "farmers and working people" (Painter, "Difference," 150). Among them, too, are "camp meeting followers, adherents of strenuous, evangelical religion, utopian communitarians, and devotees of spirit rappers and water cures" — as well as many who oppose slavery. Still, with respect to the question of salvation, they're a little on the single-minded side. They're all expecting the "literal end of the world," and "momentarily" at that, especially since they've been hearing from William Miller himself (for more than a decade by now) that the Second Advent of Christ is to take place during this very year of 1843 (146). We can infer that our speaker's tidings, whose function is to unify these "agitated" evangelicals, won't have to do with any merely human agency, just as we can infer that nobody in this stretch of the stratum can be thinking of race or gender as paramount considerations.

Let's say, therefore, that Sojourner Truth, our exemplary rhetorical agent, must, for now, be heralding an eventuality which is to sidestep race, gender, and everything else, all in one fell swoop. And let's add that she's addressing an auditor who may be described, in terms borrowed from John Newton's "Amazing Grace," as the *sanctifiable wretch*: one whose personal experience matters only as the scaffolding for salvation. Certainly, Sojourner Truth's own task can be differentiated from that of other African-American religious leaders of the day. For, while she's doing her part to link "hundreds of thousands," she's helping to enact what is, as everybody knows, a *temporary* assemblage, unlike those urban networks, those support systems for lasting social change, then under construction by sermonizers such as Samuel Eli Cornish (Painter, "Difference," 146; Hodges 2010). As a referent still circulating within the stratum of *biblical precept*, the rhetorical practitioner whom we're studying is, at present, limited to ushering everyone, regardless of their social positioning, into the divinely-constituted Liberia that will, "momentarily," be everywhere (Painter, "Difference," 146).

Crossing over to Race

We've discovered that our exemplary rhetorical agent is in no position, not as yet, to insert any "black women into women's reform" (Painter, "Difference," 140–141). But our next material-semiotic step will be to investigate another incorporeal transformation, that through which our circulating referent, long since formatted for the stratum of *biblical precept*, gradually becomes formatted for the stratum of *race* as well.

Having established a "reputation" as a "gifted preacher and singer," Sojourner Truth finds the Millerites happy to "recommend her good preaching" even to their non-Millerite "brethren" (Painter, "Difference," 146). So, through "invitations extended," Sojourner Truth starts traversing (what else but) "a Millerite network" on Long Island, crossing over from New

York, to Connecticut, and then on to Massachusetts. To be sure, it's no parting of the ways. It's just the pursuit of what Steven Johnson (1997) would call a "link" or trail of "association" (112), or what the material-semiotic researchers would call a *partial connection* — referring, actually, to the opposite of a disinterested connection (see Strathern, 1991; Mol, 2002). In any case, our exemplary rhetorical agent now follows a trail that leads, across the partial connection of preacherliness, all the way to the "utopian Northampton Association," where, "for the first time," she encounters "Garrisonian abolitionism" (Painter, "Difference," 146).

Indeed, the brethren to whom Sojourner Truth is being recommended belong to a stratum in its own right, a collectivity where religion is no "dominant relation," merely another plank in the activist's platform (Baugh 36). The activist in question might very well be a clergyman, considering that, in this second stratum, "gender" isn't so much absent as occluded. Even then, his task would be to fold salvation into social justice, not to promote it as an exit strategy. Furthermore, where Sojourner Truth is going now, the dominant relation involves not social justice in general, but abolitionism in particular. Therefore, to enter this new stratum as a bona fide participant, instead of a tourist, our exemplary rhetorical agent will have to start reinforcing the materiality of *race*, without whose political reality there couldn't, in the middle of the nineteenth century, be any concerted anti-slavery movement to begin with.

This second stratum, its inhabitants so preoccupied with skin color, is another of these alliances, networks, or cyborgs. It's a mesh within which are linked the slaves, the free black persons, and, last but not least, the anti-slavery activists — who do have to make "race" matter, if only as an expedient for liberating the slaves. For, while slavery and blackness can, in point of fact, be detached from one another (just ask any indentured Irishman of the mid-nineteenth century), the abolitionist movement of the day needs to suture them, so that the movement itself, insofar as it's a regime of signs, can lay claim to a non-ambiguous referent.

Let's now scrutinize the manner in which Sojourner Truth actually makes the transition into the stratum of *race*. She hasn't been invited on the basis of her blackness, abolitionism, femaleness, or feminism, but only because of her "good preaching" — which heretofore has been exclusively to prepare the sanctifiable wretch for the end of the world (Painter, "Difference," 146). Nevertheless, she *stays*, and for several years, at the Northampton Association, that noted hotbed of anti-slavery activism. This means that our circulating referent must, in the interim, have acquired some abolitionist credentials to go along with her millenarian qualifications.

If so, then we should be looking for the allies who make possible the integration of the preacherly Sojourner Truth into the abolitionist Northampton Association. There might be several such allies, but we'll focus on one in particular. This is David Ruggles, by now perhaps the most important "black radical abolitionist" of all, and a fixture, here in this collectivity "dedicated to antislavery issues" (Hodges 38; King, *Essence*, 137). He's "content in Northampton," where he conducts his "antislavery efforts" with the support of an entire network of "white allies" (Hodges 176, 187). He not only organizes "meetings of black Americans" but also works closely with the "white abolitionists in the area," for he's directly linked with William Lloyd Garrison (Hodges 180, 183, 185). And, yes, David Ruggles can definitely help integrate Sojourner Truth into a dominant relation to which she's never yet belonged.

It's David Ruggles who's exactly "the right person of color to help Sojourner Truth" gain some credence at Northampton (Hodges 183). It's David Ruggles, not Sojourner Truth, who has been urging "blacks to find freedom" for all these many years, and it's David Ruggles, not Sojourner Truth, who has such "very good relations with Garrison" (183). So David Ruggles will "surely" have to "approve of Truth for white abolitionists to trust her" (Hodges 184). This is because the white abolitionists will otherwise have no *reason* to trust her, not until she can show that she, too, has "embraced abolitionism" (Painter, "Difference" 147). Lest we forget, the anti-slavery activists, who have all sorts of entanglements to contend with, can simply look around to see that not all of the black people are on their team. For one thing, during the period 1790–1860, there are, in Larry Koger's (1995) turn of phrase, quite a number of "free black slave masters." For another, as David Ruggles actually reports, some of the enslaved persons themselves have been rejecting offers of enfranchisement (Hodges 187). So the abolitionists at Northampton can't expect just any African-American, not even a preacher, to be an abolitionist as well.

Yet our exemplary rhetorical agent becomes translated, and with some rapidity, into an abolitionist, starting when David Ruggles discovers in her a "potential convert to antislavery" (Hodges 183). For Ruggles exerts a "major impact on Truth's developing abolitionism," as when his "mentoring" produces some new-for-her "abolitionist views and methods" (183). Thus it comes about (in 1844, at one of these "meetings of black Americans" which Ruggles has been organizing) that Sojourner Truth, after so many years of testifying as a Methodist-and-Millenarian, makes "her first public antislavery address on the practical workings of slavery in the North" (Hodges 183–84).

From now on, Sojourner Truth is no longer just a preacher. She is, in addition, an "antislavery lecturer," and as enmeshed in the project of abolitionism as in the prospect of salvation (King, *Essence*, 137). As Deleuze and Guattari might say, it's an incorporeal transformation — a shift converting our selected speaker into a circulating referent for two different collectivities at once (ATP 88). As part of the process, Sojourner Truth has had to become black, whether or not she'd been black already. And lest it seem counterintuitive to think of Sojourner Truth as acquiring a race, we'll consult the historical record for corroboration.

For, strangely enough, Sojourner Truth emerges from the Northampton Association not only as the well-trained lecturer, but also as the "illiterate, former slave woman" (Campbell 9). Starting in the mid-1840s, she portrays herself as the unstudied innocent, just as she begins using "her body in ways" that women who are not "actresses" would never dare (Painter, "Difference," 155 ff.). She's adopted just the sort of racialized identity she'd previously have *flouted*. So this ethos of the "slave-woman victim" must have arisen from the collaboration between, on the one side, Sojourner Truth and, on the other side, the Ruggles contingent at Northampton, that training-ground not for just any activist, but for the anti-slavery activist in particular (157). Our exemplary rhetorical agent herself must have helped design a new, strategic persona, an appeal to precisely those auditors who'd be all ears for the underdog but distrustful of the revolutionary.

Yet, if this speaker is, all of a sudden, harping on her "race," it's not in the interest of anyone's personal aggrandizement. It's to render visible that very blackness, that *victimhood* of the slaves, without which abolitionism would have no discernible object. At this time, the question of race isn't a self-evident matter of fact. Instead, it's a controversial matter of concern (see Latour 2008). The abolitionists, including Sojourner Truth and David Ruggles, are among those trying to settle the controversy, which has, in the years preceding the civil war, become entangled with the metaphysics of slavery. Is slavery — as sanctioned by skin color — to be read as an evil, as a necessary evil, as a lesser evil (in comparison to emancipation), as a blessing in disguise, or what? Clearly, the abolitionists would prefer to read slavery as an evil. Yet the more pragmatic approach, at least for now, is to read slavery as an evil for the slave.

That's not the only option in town, not even among the abolitionists. For example, in his own *Narrative*, Frederick Douglass takes care to emphasize that slavery is an evil not simply for the slave, but also, believe it or not, for the slaveholder — and, by extension, for the nation to which the slaveholder belongs (see especially Chapters VI and VII). Yet, so far as concerns the abolitionists more generally, the last thing they'd need is another of these self-made men, another Frederick Douglass unwittingly to imply that any agent with enough gumption could simply emancipate himself. That's why the better strategy is to keep dramatizing that slavery, while it may yet prove an evil for the slaveholder, is definitely an evil for the close-to-hapless slave.

To say so is consistent with an explanation from the historian Nell Irvin Painter. At this time in the United States, even "free blacks" exist in "a conceptual limbo": they're "unseen or uninteresting or distasteful," plus they're too un-hapless to elicit empathy (Painter, "Difference," 154). Under the circumstances, to stand for something in particular, to acquire a clear-cut referent, the anti-slavery cause must render its object both black enough and disempowered enough to matter. If anti-slavery arguments are to take hold, then they will have to be advanced by a practitioner embodying abolitionism, blackness, and victimhood simultaneously.

At present, there aren't many candidates qualified for that role. Let's consider the predicament of Sojourner Truth's numerous "black women contemporaries in feminist abolitionism," most of them routinely overlooked, and ask, "Why this invisibility?" (Painter, "Difference," 147–48, 155–56). The answer is that they're too "free," too unvictim-like, to be seen — whether in the middle of the nineteenth century or today ("Difference," 154). And who else is available to be materializing the requisite blackness, namely, that of the slave-as-victim? It can't be the actual slaves, whose own visibility has yet to be brought into being (except, of course, when they rise up in one of these bloodbaths, these Nat Turner-style insurrections, thereby sending quite the mixed message for the anti-slavery cause).

But, during this period, "Southern" servitude does function as the very "symbol of American slavery" (Painter, *Sojourner Truth*, 8). It's the "metaphorical slave South," so "familiar…by dint of having so often been described," that encapsulates all the oppression which the Northern abolitionists are contesting, and then it's the blackness of the Southern slave that, in turn, emblematizes the metaphorical slave South (9). So there's the solution: the antislavery movement needs to come up with an envoy abolitionist enough to convey the abstractions, but victim enough — metonymically Southern enough — to literalize them, too.

And that's what the radical abolitionists, our exemplary rhetorical agent among them, do understand. It's Sojourner Truth herself who is, as one says, positioned to link the ambiguously privileged abolitionists of the North with the clearly marginalized slaves of the South. For this is a speaker who materializes the arguments of the abolitionists while also materializing the experiences of the slaves. She does so by enacting blackness-and-victimization in a newly-emergent, specifically abolitionist form, and this is how she goes about reterritorializing *race*.

Still, it's not as if Sojourner Truth is, during this next incorporeal transformation, to exchange identities, switching from highly-trained lecturer to "slave-woman victim" (Painter, "Difference," 157). It's not, for example, that she's to become "two different persons or one person divided into two" (Mol, *Body*, 80). Instead, as Annemarie Mol might observe, the subject of our investigation is to emerge as more than one but less than many (80). She'll retain her function as a circulating referent, but, from now on, it'll be for more than one collectivity at a time. As an abolitionist at home among the Christians, as a Christian at home among the abolitionists, she'll speak for the stratum of *biblical precept* and also for the stratum of *race*.

From Race to Gender

Is our exemplary practitioner henceforth empowered to say just anything among just any group of interlocutors? No, of course not, and this is because she is perceived as belonging on the *abolitionist* track of the "feminist and antislavery circuit" (Painter, *Sojourner Truth*, 171). The problem, from a material-semiotic perspective, is that she hasn't been properly formatted, at least not as a circulating referent for *gender*, for which reason she's still not positioned to enunciate anywhere near enough feminism. That's because the women's rights movement of the day is heterogeneous: some of its members embrace feminism without endorsing abolitionism. These more conservative feminists, having established a Troy of their own, are unwilling to let some abolitionist (and, by association, patriarchal) gift-horse of a Sojourner Truth into the camp.

Let's consider, as a case in point, what actually happens when, in 1850, Sojourner Truth, wandering off the abolitionist reservation, goes ahead to address a women's rights convention in Worcester, Massachusetts (see Fitch and Mandziuk 19). It's an important gathering, the "first such meeting of national scope in the United States" (Painter, *Sojourner Truth*, 114). According to the available evidence, Sojourner Truth seems to have spoken there "primarily as a preacher" (115). Yet it isn't preacherliness that saturates the fallout from her appearance.

For, in response, the conservative feminist Jane Swisshelm editorializes, in her influential *Saturday Visiter*, that "The convention was not called to discuss the rights of color, and we think it was altogether irrelevant and unwise to introduce the question" (Painter, *Sojourner Truth*, 123). There, in a nutshell, is the impasse that our exemplary practitioner is facing until 1851, when she "first" gains "prominence as a feminist" (Painter, "Difference" 140). It's as if she's become so closely affiliated with the abolitionism of the abolitionists, and with the blackness-and-victimization of the slaves, that, no matter what she says, she's heard as speaking for "the rights of color" anyway.

To appreciate the material-semiotic delicacy of the situation, let's recall that, around this time, "women" are "presumed to be white," and "blacks" are "presumed to be men" (Painter, *Sojourner Truth*, 171). But what goes for the "blacks" also goes for the abolitionists, and all the more so. It's not, as the example of the Garrisonian abolitionists might show, that the abolitionists are universally unsympathetic towards feminism; it's just that too many of them are. Indeed, the most politically-influential version of abolitionism might yet turn out to be the kind purposing to emancipate the slaves without emancipating the women. So, at present, the women's rights activists can't be sure *which* abolitionism a speaker like Sojourner Truth would bring along into the heart of their movement. That alone is enough to explain why a Jane Swisshelm would think it so "irrelevant and unwise" for the women's movement to squander its resources on the "rights of color," and all at a time when feminism still needs to territorialize itself (Painter, *Sojourner Truth*, 123).

Meanwhile, the trend within abolitionism looks to be that of alienating *gender*, and precisely as a stratagem for consolidating *race*. Regrettably, William Lloyd Garrison himself has been left marooned by the rest of the abolitionists, including within his own organization, the national Anti-Slavery Society. Thus, in 1840, with the election of three abolitionist women (Lydia Maria Child, Lucretia Mott and Maria Weston Chapman) to the executive committee of that Society, many among the abolitionist non-women have objected. Sure, they've been objecting to Garrison's uncompromising radicalism, but that's an umbrella term already covering his "support of women's rights" (Wyatt-Brown). Some of the more "religious abolitionists," those who wish to continue working through the conventional political mechanisms, have broken away to form the Liberty Party. But others have departed to form the American and Foreign Anti-Slavery Society, in which women are "denied the vote" (Venet 15). This latter, incidentally, is an organization one of whose annual reports is issued on May 6, 1851, three short weeks before Sojourner Truth gives her famous speech at the women's rights convention. In other words, just anybody at this time can see that a counter-feminist abolitionism is abroad and expanding its sphere of influence.

What's more, among the very most counter-feminist of the secessionists, those forming the American and Foreign Anti-Slavery Society, is one Samuel Eli Cornish. He's our example, mentioned above, of the various African-American activists laboring among the urban populations of the day. Now, there's no impeaching this figure (this journalist, publisher, minister, community leader) on the basis that he's lacking in the requisite abolitionist credentials. Yet it's not the moderate Liberty Party that Cornish joins after his break with the Garrisonians. Instead, and (at the very least) symbolically taking his own constituency with him, he joins the other, more conservative organization, where women are denied the vote. That's how he helps convey that not even the *black* abolitionists can automatically be expected to join the feminist team. No wonder so "many feminist abolitionists" would come "to advocate women's rights after experiencing frustration" in their antislavery work (Painter, "Difference," 148). But, then again, Samuel Eli Cornish does embody that mid-nineteenth century movement to shore up *race* by separating it from *gender*.

So far as concerns an important contingent among the beleaguered feminists, the commonsensical reaction is to respond in kind, but from the other direction (shoring up *gender* by separating it from *race*). We see this vector operating in the first-hand report of Frances Dana Gage, albeit in passages overlooked by the rhetorical theorist Karlyn Kohrs Campbell:

> old Sojourner...sat crouched against the wall...Again and again, timorous and trembling ones came to me and said with earnestness, "Don't let her speak, Mrs. G. It will ruin us. Every newspaper in the land will have our cause mixed with abolition and niggers, and we shall be utterly denounced." (Painter, *Sojourner Truth*, 167)

Despite her tendentiousness, Gage captures the dynamics accurately enough. After all, this is a time when someone like Jane Swisshelm can opt, in her editorials, to portray the women's rights movement as "a small boat in choppy waters," a vessel which "may carry woman into a safe harbor," but which "is not strong enough to bear the additional weight of all the colored men in creation" (Painter, *Sojourner Truth*, 123). From the perspective of many such feminists, the cause cannot afford any tarring with the brush of abolitionism.

But this, in the period just before her famous speech, looks inauspicious for Sojourner Truth, who becomes quite the locus of anxiety. Following "her stay at Northampton," her "name" has started "appearing sporadically in newspapers," but only "as an antislavery lecturer" (King, *Essence*, 137). That's her label in 1850, at the Old Colony Anti-Slavery Society meeting in Plymouth, Massachusetts (Fitch and Mandziuk 18). As for those newspapers, they do include the *Liberator*, the *Anti-Slavery Bugle*, and the *National Anti-Slavery Standard* (Campbell 11, 17). That's because she's "actively" working with "many abolitionists," including on "tours for the American Anti-Slavery Society" (Fitch and Mandziuk 18). For example, she appears, with "other distinguished abolitionists," on an "antislavery" lecturing "tour" in Western New York (Painter, *Sojourner Truth*, 116). And when she addresses an audience in March, 1851 (immediately before rematerializing at the women's rights gathering in Akron), it's an "antislavery convention" that she's attending. So, yes, everybody understands what Sojourner

Truth has been doing for abolitionism. But nobody can tell what she might yet do to feminism.

At this juncture — between 1850 and 1851 — there's a choice for the women's rights activists more generally. It's either to collaborate with an alliance between the radical abolitionists (Sojourner Truth included) and the anti-slavery feminists, an alliance tainted, after all, rather more insidiously by the invisible privilege of the patriarchs than by the visible blackness of the slaves. Or else it's to trust in a conservative feminism that takes *women's* interests to heart. For, while the abolitionists can't expect just any black person to be good for abolitionism, the feminists can't expect just any black person to be good for women's rights.

Earlier, we've found that it must certainly have taken some allies to facilitate Sojourner Truth's incorporeal transformation from an apocalyptic into an abolitionist. Now we'll notice a parallel with respect to her production as a feminist, and specifically of the kind that can insert "black women into women's reform" (Painter, "Difference," 140). Clearly, this speaker's rhetorical agency must be contingent upon, heritable from whichever pathways she follows into the women's movement. Yet the difference between Sojourner Truth's rhetorical agency in 1850, when she's rebuffed by the bona fide feminists, and in 1851, when she's accepted by them, is finally a matter of scale. In 1850, her rhetorical agency, though as real as ever before, isn't so big or important in the stratum of *gender* as it is elsewhere. But in 1851, the speaker is not only a religious activist, and an antislavery activist, but a women's rights activist, too. This means that somebody or something must, in the interim, have hooked her up, helping rescale what remains, nonetheless, her own rhetorical agency.

For how is it, according to the material-semiotic perspective, that agency can ever be resized, or an agent made equal to a task of which she isn't already capable? The answer is that scale is always the "achievement" of the actors themselves, since "action," a "property of associated entities," is always performed by "Agent 1 plus Agent 2 plus Agent 3" (Latour, *Reassembling*, 185; *Pandora's* 182).

Rescaling the Envoy

If we scrutinize the activity currently taking place around our exemplary rhetorical agent, we find that the support system for rescaling (and redistributing) her rhetorical agency comprises quite a number of disparate actors, practices, and artifacts. Not all of these are purposing to maximize the rhetorical agency of Sojourner Truth. Yet, in collaborating to create a bridge between *race* and *gender*, many of them are resizing that rhetorical agency, anyway. For simplicity, let's consider the material-semiotic roles played, first, by one exemplary actor, second, by one exemplary practice, and, finally, by one exemplary artifact.

We'll identify the exemplary actor as Parker Pillsbury, who, right around 1850, is known all over the Northwest as a minister and social reformer. In addition to his abolitionism, he's fully involved in the women's rights movement, which is why he can eventually help draft the constitution of the feminist American Equal Rights Association (1865), and serve as vice-president of the New Hampshire Woman Suffrage Association, and — with Elizabeth Cady Stanton — co-edit the women's rights newsletter *The Revolution*. At this moment, though, we're interested in Pillsbury's functionality as an actor transporting Sojourner Truth's rhetorical agency into the stratum of *gender*. It's a reminder that agency can be constrained and enabled by one and the same mechanism. For Pillsbury's response to the conservative feminists is to reframe, to remediate, what's just happened in 1850, at that women's rights convention in Worcester, where Sojourner Truth has wandered off the circuit's abolitionist track. He does so in the very pages of Jane Swisshelm's newspaper, that mechanism for separating *gender* from *race*.

To recognize that Pillsbury's contribution counts as an event, a material-semiotic achievement, let's link that intervention to a pairing of concepts from rhetorical studies proper. Specifically, let's read Pillsbury, in his commentary on the fallout from the Worcester convention of 1850, as *turning the tables* on Swisshelm and her followers, leaving them saddled with the *burden of proof* — exactly as if they (in proposing that the rights of black women henceforth be excluded from the rights of women) are the ones calling for the unwarranted innovation. After all, or so Pillsbury insinuates, the default position, the status quo for abolitionists and feminists alike, is that the rights of colored women are necessarily included in the rights of women. And now, all of a sudden, here's this disruptive proposal, from Swisshelm et al., that we start fixing something that isn't broken, as by showing these "colored" ladies the door (Painter, *Sojourner Truth*, 123). So that's how to interpret the interchange taking place between Pillsbury and Swisshelm, late in the year 1850, and in the pages of the *Saturday Visiter*. It's the emergence and resolution of a controversy as to who it really is that's advocating the needless departure from the way that things already are.

Yet Pillsbury is now writing into the record a state of affairs more self-evident than it may seem: "That any woman has rights, will be scarcely believed. But that colored women have rights, would never have been thought of, without a specific declaration" (Painter, *Sojourner Truth*, 123). All that's happened at Worcester, on Pillsbury's account, is that someone has finally gone ahead and uttered a "specific" articulation, an innocent "declaration," a Deleuzean enunciation of that feminist-and-abolitionist truth, all aimed at a general public that simply wouldn't have "thought of" it. Certainly, there's been no introduction, into the woman question, of the color question. Instead, there's been an unfolding of the latter from the former.

So, by writing the state of affairs into the record to begin with, Pillsbury is, in effect, constituting a trajectory for abolitionism and feminism to share. He's placing a chronotopic stepping stone just a little ahead of Sojourner Truth, making possible another of her incorporeal transformations. He's paving her way from Worcester, where she's been rebuffed as a mere spokesperson for race, to Akron, where she's to emerge, in addition, as a feminist, that is, as a circulating referent for gender. His interference then facilitates a *multiple* territorialization, simultaneously of abolitionism (spreading into the women's rights movement) and of feminism (infiltrating the anti-slavery cause).

But it's time for us to consider the material-semiotic role of just one exemplary practice. This latter might not sound like much, for it's simply that of participating, in the middle of the nineteenth century, at women's rights meetings. Yet a practice which facilitates a link between abolitionism and feminism needn't be dismissed as trivial. In this case, the practice gains much of its specificity from the interaction between our exemplary rhetorical agent and one Marius Robinson. Robinson, both a clergyman and a noted abolitionist, is not only the editor of the *Anti-Slavery Bugle* but also, together with his wife Emily, the personal friend and host of Sojourner Truth (Baker; Painter, *Sojourner Truth*, 119). Besides, like Parker Pillsbury, Robinson has been acquiring some feminist credentials of his own. That's how he can help create the conditions under which Sojourner Truth may give her speech in the first place.

What's remarkable, though, is that our exemplary rhetorical agent seems, as of 1850, to be reacting with surprise at the prospect that she, an abolitionist lecturer, might be able to participate in the women's rights movement as well:

> Truth learned of the May 28, 1851, Ohio women's rights convention in Akron from Robinson. The subject interested her. She had spoken at the 1850 women's rights conference in Worcester, Massachusetts. (King 137)

So, at this very moment (even as she's being criticized, in the feminist press, for her unsanctioned appearance at Worcester), our protagonist is discussing her nascent feminism, not with just anybody, but with a fellow abolitionist, Marius Robinson, who invites her to an important women's rights convention at which he himself will be the secretary.

It's not, of course, that Robinson is the only actor to have helped articulate Sojourner Truth with the practice of speaking up at women's rights meetings. We might adduce the role played by none other than Frances Dana Gage. She officiated as president for the convention in Akron, and she granted our exemplary rhetorical agent permission to speak, and she published the fictive rendition of the speech which is, by now, "more frequently cited" than the Robinson version (Campbell 17). Still, the main inference to draw is that, in the middle of the nineteenth century, even to *encourage* someone's participation at women's rights meetings can be to help materialize her rhetorical agency.

What remains to be clarified is why there should be any difference between the outcome of Sojourner Truth's practice in 1850, when she risks a journalistic drubbing from conservatives like Jane Swisshelm, and that of her practice in 1851, when she goes back to speak before an audience once again including the Swisshelm contingent. Oughtn't the practice lead to much the same results in each instance? Well, no: this second time, the practice will be operationalized not by the under-scaled sort of agent who jumped the track at Worcester, but, instead, by an upgraded agent who is supported — indeed, transported — by her allies. Just as it's taken certain actors and practices to convert her into a spokesperson first for salvation and second for abolitionism, it now takes certain others to convert her into a spokesperson for women's rights as well. These others include, as we've seen, the abolitionist-and-feminist Marius Robinson, who is ensuring that Sojourner Truth gain a hearing among the feminists, certainly those whose testimony he'll record in his role as secretary. So Robinson is, in effect, carrying our exemplary rhetorical agent along in her transition from *race* to *gender*, making it possible for her, in the long run, to insert "black women into women's reform" (Painter, *Sojourner Truth*, 140).

Having considered the contributions (to Sojourner Truth's most recent incorporeal transformation) of just one actor and just one practice, we can address the contribution of just one artifact. Frankly, the selection of an artifact will be arbitrary, though we're guided to our choice by no less than Campbell's (2005) canonical essay on rhetorical agency. There, we learn that Sojourner Truth's most "famous line" echoes "a recurring theme," of "women's antislavery discourse, where "female slaves" are "given voice" through the question, "Am I not a woman and a sister?" (Campbell 12, 17). Campbell underlines the point by referring us to the illustration of an "antislavery token" from 1838. If we retrace her steps, cycling back to Phillip Lapansky's "Graphic Discord" (1994), we find close to thirty comparable depictions, all having to do with female slaves. They come from the pages of books and broadsides, and from etchings and engravings and woodcuts and lithographs, and even from the surface of a pin cushion. But the artifact on which we'll concentrate, situating it not as unanchored signification but as circulating reference, is the anti-slavery token.

We find that the artifact reads "AM I NOT A WOMAN & A SISTER," and that it features the image of a "female supplicant": a slave who is kneeling, clasping her hands, looking upward in prayer (Lapansky 206, 208; also see Campbell 18, Painter, "Difference," 156, and King 139). In the nineteenth century, this figure would be accompanied by "the writings of early female activists," a category emphatically including "African Americans" (Lapansky 206). Additionally, she and her affiliated supplicants

> adorned countless abolitionist books, pamphlets, newspapers, periodicals, broadsides, letterheads, and printed ephemera. They were also replicated in handicraft goods and even…chinaware, tokens, linen, and silk goods sold by the antislavery women at their annual fund-raising fairs.

So it turns out that the anti-slavery token, together with all sorts of other co-constituents, is indeed participating in a material-semiotic network. The latter is an alliance, an assemblage in which antislavery tokens and silk goods are folded into practices (like that of holding annual fund-raising fairs), practices which are, in turn, operationalized by actors (such as antislavery women). And what is it that all these moveable parts are accomplishing? Well, at the very least, they're producing an *agencement* — an agency — for translating an abolitionist into a feminist. Even the antislavery token, by helping to enact some commensurability between the interests of the abolitionists and the interests of the feminists, is helping to format Sojourner Truth for the stratum of *gender*.

And A'n't We a Meshwork?

When Sojourner Truth does come to speak at the women's rights convention of 1851, she will (constitutively) be knotting together such filaments as are already there. That's her role in materializing an incorporeal transformation so massive that, as a result, the sanctifiable wretches, the abolitionists, the feminists, the slaves who are "presumed to be men," the clearly female supplicants, the whole lot of them together, can belong to a single, heterogeneous collectivity (Painter, *Sojourner Truth*, 171). True, it's only while we are in the material-semiotic landscape that we can see things this way. For we're in a world whose imperative is to make materiality matter, rather than let it disappear into subjectivity, or conventionality, or transcendence.

From a material-semiotic perspective, then, it proves quite manageable to explain how Sojourner Truth's (triangulable if hypothetical) speech of 1851 would actually work. We know there's a central claim—namely, that the speaker is a woman's rights activist—accompanied by a cluster of themes and images: *biblical precept, race, gender,* and all the rest. So we could unfold the functionality of the speech simply by revisiting, connecting, and (not to forget) separating the kinds of arguments adumbrated in the preceding chapters.

For the sake of illustration, let's notice that adopting such a perspective would readily allow us to study the manner in which, say, rhetorical subjectivity might be reconfigured with the aid of rhetorical conventionality. We could, for example, begin with the shared value of Christian love, which could be shown finally to connect Sojourner Truth with practically all of the key players (radicals and conservatives alike) among the abolitionists and feminists of the mid-nineteenth century (see Bogin and Yellin, 1994; Painter, 1994; King, 2006).

But the main stipulation, in this or any other material-semiotic endeavor, would be for us to flatten our ontology, and all the way down. That's how the salient co-constituents of rhetorical agency (i.e., subjectivity, conventionality, transcendence, and materiality) and also the salient participants in rhetorical transaction (e.g., Christian love, Sojourner Truth, abolitionism, antislavery tokens, feminism) could surface not as alternative proxies for some underlying social logic, but, instead, as irreducible, unassimilable equals.

However, we might go further yet, pushing our material-semiotic perspective so very far that, undergoing its own incorporeal transformation, it emerges as an assemblage-theoretical vision proper. It'd be well worth our while to understand how the rhetorical transaction we've been investigating (Sojourner Truth's triangulable if hypothetical speech of 1851) might involve the shifting of *terms* into a new *relation*. Meanwhile, it'd be no merely arbitrary choice to settle on the material-semiotic approach as the best of the four candidates for theoretical development. That's because, under present conditions, the other options (i.e., the social-structural, the rhetorical-humanistic, and the existential-transversal) are colonizing one another, with all of their terms and relations appearing increasingly isotopic. We've seen as much in Campbell's canonical essay of 2005, where rhetorical agency looks to be not only promiscuous, but also protean, paradoxical, and paper-thin. In short, it's in the material-semiotic landscape alone that terms and relations can be described thickly enough to stay separable.

So, in anticipation of an ending, we'll return to that condition of diremption, or triremption (discussed in the chapter on the existential-humanistic version of rhetorical agency) where the salient terms are (white) *man*, (black) *slave*, and (white) *woman*. Now, if Sojourner Truth is to insert black women into women's reform, she'll have to find some rhetorical means for (a) extracting these terms out of any relations that have been keeping them apart, and for (b) transporting them into a relation where they're indisputably drawn together. What, then, would be an assemblage-theoretical explanation for the manner in which the protagonist proceeds?

In her speech of 1851, our exemplary rhetorical agent is constitutively (that is, productively) shifting the three terms into very different relations than before. On the one front, leaving *woman* where it is, she makes *slave* matter as a near-synonym for *woman*, with the result that the blackness of the slave-victim counts as an attribute of the woman-victim, too. On the other front, leaving *slave* where it is, she makes *man* matter as a near synonym for *sanctifiable wretch*, so that abolitionism proper, increasingly purified of its association with patriarchy, takes on an association with salvation instead. Henceforth, the terms *slave* and *man* can belong to Christianity, to abolitionism, and to feminism, too — since the religion as such (with its presumption that we, the lot of us, are in perpetual need of redemption) does stretch out to include so many of the women's rights activists to begin with.

By now, if Sojourner Truth is coming along to say that she — a preacher, a (former) slave, a black person, and an abolitionist — is a woman, or a woman's rights, then she is bringing along with her, into the heart of gender, not only the *sanctifiable wretch* and the black, victimized *slave*, but also the increasingly redeemable *man*. So it's true that our exemplary rhetorical agent is inserting "black women into women's reform" (Painter, *Sojourner Truth*, 140). But that's not the half of it. She's also inserting white men, and black men, and Christians into women's reform. For, in this altered dominant relation, "woman" itself is becoming realized, enacted, materialized as a hybrid, so that everybody can have a chance to enter the fold, joining the movement for women's rights. Yes, it's like Spartacus, with the difference that there's no colossally authentic individual in sight. There's only an internally-heterogeneous assemblage, an alliance where subjectivities (or identities), shared values, existential claims, original bodies, agents, practices, artifacts can, all of them, play a part.

When we adopt an assemblage-theoretical (*including* material-semiotic) approach, we no longer need to generate rhetorical agency by fiat. Instead, we can study rhetorical agency as a network effect (a production of the cyborg, by the alliance, for the assemblage). Even so, there is an important observation to add with regard to the material-semiotic perspective, though applicable to the social-structural and rhetorical-humanistic perspectives, too. This is that not even what Nathan Stormer (2009) has called the will to matter can explain *why* (rather than how) it matters if some exemplary rhetorical agent ever does help to build certain materialities, or to deploy certain shared values, or to (re)constitute certain subjectivities, thereby making things otherwise than they are. The very question returns us to the problem of the rhetorical agent, whether construed as a structural subject, a whole person, an existential self, an ineffable participant, or something else. Let's keep it in mind during the next chapter, which concludes our investigation into a four-folded and traveling rhetorical agency.

7.
Agency in the Rhetorical-Theoretical World

THE PRECEDING STUDY has taken us into four distinct landscapes of rhetorical agency. These discrete paradigms are theoretical-and-practical workspaces for the production of subjectivity, of conventionality, of transcendence, and of materiality. While each locale does offer an indispensible contribution to our thinking about rhetorical agency (highlighting structural constraints, or shared values, or authentic claims, or variegated networks), each models the rhetorical agent in its own, proprietary way. So, although there are several options for theorizing the connection between rhetorical transaction and genuine social change, the choices aren't, all of them, available in the same place.

In the social-structural landscape, rhetorical subjectivity is being assembled out of terms that always dissolve into their relations. The rhetorical agent is a structural subject perpetually reproducing its own "unavoidable" condition (Campbell 3). It's an agent quite incapable, other than by theoretical fiat, of speaking in such a way as to make any difference, an agent attached as closely to the state as is a barnacle to a ship. But, then again, the interiority of speakers and listeners cannot be other than collectively contextualized. For that reason, it's perfectly appropriate for there to be a social-structural paradigm, where the local theorists and practitioners can continue manufacturing all manner of constraints upon the structural subject.

In the rhetorical-humanistic landscape, rhetorical conventionality is being assembled out of at least some terms that don't merge with their relations. True, the rhetorical agent is a whole person, routinely finessing certain traditionally-held values that come from who knows where. Nevertheless, in deploying such guidelines, the whole person can promote some genuine social change, if only by helping the group recover its longed-for coherence. Thus we should applaud the existence of the rhetorical-humanistic world, whose inhabitants do keep producing a form of rhetorical conventionality serviceable enough for any whole person to keep redirecting.

Meanwhile, in the existential-transversal landscape, rhetorical transcendence is being assembled primarily out of terms that don't reduce to their relations. For better or worse, the rhetorical agent is the existential self, reducing half to lack, loss, or absence, and half to quite the occasionalist corporeality. To be sure, the occasionalist half might yet give up the ghost, now that there is no longer any "self-sufficient agency that can qualify as intentional," and now that "choice" is "objectively co-caused at the crossroads of chance and determinacy (Massumi, qtd. in Hall 120). Even so, the existential self does give *itself* "reasons" for being, regardless that it doesn't initially "have" any (Beauvoir 12). That's justification enough for us not merely to cherish but actually to rehabilitate the existential-transversal landscape, the only world in which an existential self could thrive to begin with.

In the material-semiotic landscape, rhetorical materiality is being assembled entirely out of terms that remain separable from their relations. The rhetorical agent is an ineffable participant, forever making things otherwise than they are, and yet forever morphing into all sorts of other ineffable participants. Nobody here can say exactly why any of this activity should be going on, or under what circumstances (or to what extent) it should ever be stopped. So it does appear that the ineffable participant of this landscape ought to stay in close communication with the existential self from the other, existential-transversal world. This would be so that the former sort of agent can sometimes borrow, from the latter, the "reasons" that neither could possibly have in the first place (Beauvoir 12). However, its ethical slightness notwithstanding, the material-semiotic perspective does warrant our protection, since it's a preserve for all the resources empowering the ineffable participant to materialize everything, even transcendence.

So it's not only that each of the four landscapes persists, each in its own way, as a factory for producing a four-folded rhetorical agency. It's also that each persists despite the persistence of its others. Meanwhile, there's no theoretical justification for stapling such paradigms together. To the contrary, it's incumbent upon us to inculcate the incommensurability among the four perspectives, so that rhetorical agency can stay irreducibly four-folded.

Now, one might think, given the sophistication with which rhetorical functionality is being studied, that we're cognizant enough of the complexity, the reputed perversity of rhetorical agency. Yet rhetorical agency is becoming *less* multiple all the time. For theory seems bent on suturing the landscapes, on assembling a certain rhetorical world, on manufacturing a singular — Thomas Rickert (2013) would prefer "ambient" — home for all four types of rhetorical agent simultaneously. That's the blueprint for a concentration camp, its blended atmosphere too toxic for any meeting among the ineffable participant, the existential self, the whole person, and the structural subject, all of whom do need to be left in their own ontologies.

No More Homogenization Now!

Let's underline the exigency by examining some of the recent work on rhetorical materiality, reading the results in the manner of a cautionary tale. After all, as we've seen in our travels, rhetorical materiality is already folded into rhetorical agency, for which reason the ongoing effacement of rhetorical materiality — or, alternatively, the suturing of the material-semiotic landscape to its others — can serve as an allegory for what's happening to the rest of rhetorical agency as well. So we'll reflect on two equally sophisticated contributions. One affirms that rhetorical practices should certainly be conceptualized as materially irreducible. The other affirms that our thinking about rhetorical functionality has certainly moved beyond the naive view in which any tangible signifier can only ever be the figure (the notionally material trace), while ideology must always be the constitutive ground. Nevertheless the very authors advancing these claims are among those currently assembling a single rhetorical world, a concentration camp for all sorts of theorists and practitioners at once.

Here's the contribution of Ronald Walter Greene, a scholar who "perhaps more than any other" is "committed to thinking the problem of rhetoric's materiality" (Trapani 344). In an essay of 1998, Greene chastises Michael Calvin McGee for having developed a "fragmentation thesis" that effectively "keeps a materialist rhetoric locked into a logic of representation" (34). McGee's claim is that the rhetorical utterances around us must surely mirror the fragmentation that characterizes our multiply distributed sociality more generally. In that case, as Greene explains, McGee's error is to have inculcated a view in which

> Rhetorical practices do not exhibit their own positivity, their own unique place in the structure of everyday life, their materiality does not resist but simply reflects what we already know: that we live in a fragmented culture. (34)

We may discern the prescience of Ronald Walter Greene when we grasp that the complaint still applies today, and to no less than the approach promoted by Ronald Walter Greene.

To be sure, Greene (1998; 2009) has become adamant as to the sheer pointlessness, in theorizing rhetorical materiality, of invoking concepts like representation, influence, coercion, suspicion, and so on. He maintains that power operates autonomously, silently, through constitutive-and-productive articulations, in short, *materially*, rather than at the level of ideation. But let's note a rejoinder from William Trapani, which is that Greene himself, in one of his works, "inadvertently smuggles in an unreconstructed notion of communication as mediation and thus risks losing the very prospect of a new 'materialist rhetoric'" (Trapani 345). Whether inadvertently or otherwise, Greene does persist in reinstating the very notion of representation (communication, mediation, and so on) that he has so vociferously contested.

For example, Greene (2009) is the one who can continue to write, and always about rhetorical materialism, passages like this, wherein rhetoric's materiality is framed as that of some delivery system, dutifully channeling the interests of the status quo: "The need to govern the rhetorical subject is due to how a generalized rhetoricality infuses capitalism with its dynamic energy to produce and appropriate the social wealth of communicative labor" (61). So, in Greene, rhetorical materiality isn't irreducible, after all. It's reducible to capitalism's needy automatism. Although capitalism is nowadays governing the subject by other-than-symbolistic means, it's still expressing itself perfectly, if not through signification, then through the rhetorical materiality that it's so definitively appropriated.

Here, the point is that even if Greene is correct (about theory's need to acknowledge rhetoric's irreducible positivity), it wouldn't yet help for him to be correct, since not even Greene is clear as to how rhetorical materiality could resist, rather than simply reflect, what we already know. In this instance, we can be sure we're living in a capitalist society. And *that*, according to Greene, is what rhetorical materiality tells us, too! But where, in that case, is rhetoric's material difference, its irreducible heterogeneity?

Maybe it's in the contribution of Christian Lundberg, also representative of the scholars committed to thinking the problem of rhetoric's materiality. In his "On Missed Encounters: Lacan and the Materiality of Rhetoric" (2009), Lundberg characterizes the two most salient versions of "the materiality of rhetoric thesis" as inadequate (162). Theorizing about rhetorical materiality, he says, has led to certain "advances," but these don't quite register the "irreducible plurality and specificity of rhetorical events, texts, and practices" (161, 163). One of the advances has been "beyond an object-centered view of rhetoric as durable effect against an ideational bias" and "toward an ever more expansive view of discourse constituting the subject" (163). Another has been "beyond the critical categories of representation and interpretation" and "toward attention to logics of power and articulation that produce reality." But that's not all there is to the advances.

In Lundberg's view, the latest advance looks to be that of folding the other two advances together, as by recruiting "articulation theory" to serve as a "principle" of order — a principle "mediating the divide between the order of discourse and the order of reality by reading them as simultaneous" (Lundberg 163). And what bothers Lundberg is the seamlessness presupposed in this convergence, hence his lamentation that the two advances, especially when blended, can only conduce to the effacement of rhetoric's "irreducible plurality and specificity" (161).

By reading Lundberg a little against the grain, we begin to see that he's protesting too much. In celebrating the advance "beyond an object-centered view of rhetoric as durable effect" he himself is dismissing the possibility that objects, things, corporealities might yet have some materiality of their own (Lundberg 163). For him, it's not even the object, only talk about the object that matters. Meanwhile, in celebrating the advance "beyond the critical categories of representation and interpretation," he himself is dismissing the possibility that signification can matter, either (161). For he's the one agreeing that the "logics of power and articulation" can "produce reality" all by themselves, i.e., that it's no longer meaningful to differentiate between the map and the territory (163). So *of course* to fold together the two advances is to leave out any irreducible plurality and specificity. It's to render everything (events, texts, practices, objects, durable effects, and so on) epiphenomenal to an all-encompassing social totality.

But what is Lundberg's own suggestion for re-admitting rhetoric's irreducible plurality, specificity, and heterogeneity? Well, it's to refer rhetorical materiality to a linguistic loop. Technically, the argument is that rhetoric remains material because, on the one side, rhetoric is animated by a material drive that operates out of awareness, and because, on the other side, rhetoric is the material trace left in signification — insinuated into "practice" — by the material drive itself (Lundberg 162).

To begin with, there would appear to be two sorts of material available for reworking by the material drive. But the one sort is linguistic, comprising such symbolizations as are continually reconfigured during the ordinary, trope-deploying processes of communicative interchange. And the other sort is linguistic, too, comprising the extraordinary content of the unconscious, which is only the "reservoir of all the possible metonymic associations potentially inhering in a signifier by way of past usage" (171). So far, Lundberg's rhetorical materiality is divided neatly between tropes which are familiar because they're new, and tropes which are uncanny because they're old. Of course, there's still the question of the material drive that's *animating* these processes of signification. Oddly, not even the material drive can matter. Its functionality is limited to that of reshuffling all those representations, some of them brand-new, the remainder second-hand.

Thus the approaches of Greene and of Lundberg are comparably flawed, though in opposite directions. Greene theorizes rhetorical materiality too reductively (as whatever might be left after the vacuuming-out of all linguisticality), and Lundberg theorizes rhetorical materiality too expansively (as whatever might turn out, once again, to be linguisticality in disguise). Either way, rhetorical materiality, like all the rest of rhetorical agency, is theorized in a manner that effaces its internal heterogeneity.

On Keeping Difference Different

In reflecting on what both Greene and Lundberg have to say, we can still arrive at a couple of clues as to where to find rhetoric's disappearing heterogeneity. The clue from Lundberg is that rhetoric *should* be theorized as speaking with the aid of such objects, things, corporealities as are "durable" enough to stick in the gears of any social machine bent on generating everything in its image (163). Indeed, to trivialize the durable and the object-oriented, as by moving beyond them, would be a step in the wrong direction. We should therefore, as even Lundberg suggests, consider rolling back this notion that rhetorical materiality can somehow be captured in a reading of "the order of discourse and the order of reality...as simultaneous." Similarly, the clue from Greene is that rhetoric *should* be theorized as speaking with its own, resistant positivity (always telling us something different from what we already know), even if Greene hasn't actually theorized it that way.

Indeed, the problem uncovered above may be simply that the rhetorical theorists keep forgetting where they are. Perhaps, for example, Lundberg and Greene have come to think they're wandering around the one rhetorical world, when they're actually perambulating within the social-structural perspective (an environment-and-imperative where rhetorical subjectivity is the dominant term, and everything else a satellite). Perhaps these writers are trying to study rhetorical materiality with the aid of resources which are only good for studying rhetorical subjectivity. Perhaps this sort of misprision could be minimized were more of the local theorists to take seriously the commitments ordering their own, provincial paradigm.

Yet the four alternative frameworks are already there, even if they do have to be understood in their own terms. Any attempt to blenderize them, or to staple them together, would be rhetorical-theoretical imperialism. Let's, therefore, leave the landscapes alone, so that all those local theorists and practitioners can keep making their idiosyncratic contributions to a four-folded rhetorical agency. But, in that case, if the four paradigms ought indeed to be kept apart, we're left with the question as to how resources from all four of them, crossing the abysses between, could ever become reconciled in rhetorical transaction.

A Fluctuating Rhetorical Agent

Perhaps we could assemble a theorist-and-practitioner of quite another stripe, a participant who's capable of bringing some radical alterity into each and every landscape, even when the locals aren't up to the task. We could add a fifth figure to the list of those belonging to the category of "rhetorical agent," arriving at a metaphor, at a model for the interlocutor on call. Holding a quadruple passport, claiming citizenship in all quarters of the rhetorical-theoretical world, she could show up in any of the perspectives, always importing tidings from elsewhere.

A traveler like that could draw any local agent's attention to connections (as between here and there), to linkages that, if not for her reminding presence, might seem impossible to detect. These would remain partial connections, as Marilyn Strathern (1991) or Annemarie Mol (2002) would say, and therefore partial separations, too. But they'd still be connections. Doubtless, such a traveling rhetorical agent would be a messenger, an ontological drifter, maybe a sophist. And there is just such a model in the work of Michel Serres, the ally of so many a material-semiotic theorist. He has a book about it — *Angels: A Modern Myth* (1995). As for the angels populating the book, they're of the kind that "fluctuates between the collective and the individual," bearing "relationships" (293, 295).

Admittedly, the angels haven't yet borne *enough* relationships. Often, they've settled for bearing only selective, elitist relationships, those echoed in "the cry in the desert," in "the burning prophecy or the psalm," in "the rustling of crossed wings," in "the coded message, transported, delivered, received and deciphered," in "emphatic words and speeches," in "written law, sign, meaning," in "the signified and the signifier," in "speech, language, commentary and interpretation" (Serres 284). So the angel of the past — and here one might think of the steganographic angel posited, in the fifteenth century, by Johannes Trithemius (see Kolata), or of the mediological angel adduced so much more recently (see Debray) — wouldn't have been such a good model for any traveling rhetorical agent.

Yes, but even the angels are undergoing remediation. They are becoming freed up to traverse all manner of "paths" and "interlacings," and their work is now that of "unceasingly drawing up the maps of our new universe" (Serres 293). Indeed, they're heralding the annunciation, when "word" becomes "flesh" (295). This is no idle auspication. For, as Serres implies elsewhere, communication needn't continue reducing to some (let's say, Kantian, Husserlian, Sartrean) tomb for a "petrified linguistic body," its "tongue and nostrils parched with dialectic," or even to some perseverative ritual whereby the referent keeps disappearing into the signified (Connor 162).

The way that Serres actually puts it, though, is that the angels, the fluctuating, relationship-bearing angels coming up today, are

> individual and multiple; messengers that both appear and disappear; visible and invisible; constructive of messages and message-bearing systems...spiritual and physical; of two sexes and none; natural and manufactured; collective and social; both orderly and

> disorderly...intermediaries and interchangers; intelligence that can be found in the world's objects and artefacts. (296)

Come to think of it, that's what we've been hearing all along. We've been hearing it from our exemplary rhetorical agent, the preacher who's accompanied us from beginning to end, bearing with her those difficult relationships that produce a four-folded rhetorical agency.

So there's a model, a metaphor. With our help, the traveling rhetorical agent, that fluctuating angel, might come to collect all of the items on agency's checklist, filling her knapsack with unassimilable supplies, bundling these into the form of the communicative artifact. Her own speech would be a gift for carrying around, for unfolding within any collectivity susceptible to the rhetorical will to matter. After all, while humans can't be the only agents in town, they still need assistance in their own right. And what else, if not the intervention of their allies, could impel them to make things otherwise?

Works Cited

Akrich, Madeleine, and Bruno Latour. "A Summary of a Convenient Vocabulary for the Semiotics of Human and Nonhuman Assemblies." *Shaping Technology/Building Society: Studies in Sociotechnical Change*. Eds. Wiebe E. Bijker and John Law. Cambridge: MIT Press, 1992.

Anton, Corey, and Valerie P. Peterson. "Who Said What: Subject Positions, Rhetorical Strategies, and Good Faith." *Communication Studies* 54.4 (2003): 403–419.

Aristotle. *On Rhetoric: A Theory of Civic Discourse*. Trans. George Kennedy. 2nd ed. New York: Oxford UP, 2007.

Baker, J. "An Abolitionist Tarred and Feathered." *Times-Reporter* [New Philadelphia, Ohio], 18 July 2008. Web. 29 May 2013.

Barker, Robert L. "Normative." *The Social Work Dictionary*. 3rd ed. Washington, DC: NASW, 1995.

Baugh, Bruce. "Body." Paar 35–37.

Barnett, Richard Scot. "A Space for Agency: Rhetorical Agency, Spatiality, and the Production of Relations in Supermodernity." MA thesis. North Carolina State University, 2005. Web. 17 April 2012.

Beauvoir, Simone de. *The Ethics of Ambiguity*. [Trans. B. Frechtman]. New York: Citadel, 1948.

Benítez Bribiesca, Luis. "Memetics: A Dangerous Idea." *Interciencia.* 26.1 (2001): 29–31. Web. 22 June 2012.

Biesecker, Barbara A. "Rethinking the Rhetorical Situation from Within the Thematic of Différance." *Contemporary Rhetorical Theory: A Reader*. Eds. John Louis Lucaites, Celeste Michelle Condit, and Sally Caudill. New York: Guilford, 1999. 232–246.

Biesecker, Barbara A., and John Louis Lucaites, eds. *Rhetoric, Materiality, and Politics*. New York: Peter Lang, 2009.

Blumenberg, Hans. "An Anthropological Approach to the Contemporary Significance of Rhetoric." *After Philosophy: End or Transformation?* Trans. Robert M. Wallace. Ed. Kenneth Baynes, James Bohman, and Thomas McCarthy. Cambridge: MIT Press, 1987.

Bogin, Ruth, and Jean Fagan Yellin. "Introduction." Yellin and Van Horne 1–19. Brockriede, Wayne. "Arguers as Lovers." *Philosophy and Rhetoric* 5 (1972): 1–11. Bryant, Donald C. "Rhetoric: Its Functions and Its Scope." Quarterly Journal of Speech 39 (1953): 401–424.

Burke, Kenneth. *Permanence and Change: An Anatomy of Purpose*. Berkeley: UC Press, 1984.

Butler, Judith. "Performativity's Social Magic." *Bourdieu: A Critical Reader*. Ed. Richard Shusterman. Malden: Blackwell, 1999.

Callon, Michel. "Some Elements of a Sociology of Translation: Domestication of the Scallops and the Fishermen of St. Brieuc Bay." *Power, Action and Belief: A New Sociology of Knowledge?* Ed. John Law. London: Routledge, 1986. 196–223.

Campbell, Karlyn Kohrs. "Agency: Promiscuous and Protean." *Communication and Critical/Cultural Studies* 2.1 (2005): 1–19.

Card, Claudia, ed. *The Cambridge Companion to Simone de Beauvoir*. New York: Cambridge UP, 2003.

Cherwitz, Richard, ed. *Rhetoric and Philosophy*. New York: Routledge, 1990. Coates, Paul. "Sense Data." *Internet Encyclopedia of Philosophy*. 6 June 2007. Web. 18 April 2012.

Colebrook, Claire. "Introduction." Paar 1–7.

Connor, Steven. "Michel Serres's *Les Cinq Sens*." *Mapping Michel Serres*. Ed. Niran Abbas. Ann Arbor: U of Michigan P, 2005.

Cooper, Marilyn M. "Rhetorical Agency as Emergent and Enacted." CCC 62:3 (2011): 420–449.

Crowley, Sharon. "Response to Karlyn Kohrs Campbell, 'Agency.'" Alliance of Rhetoric Societies Convention. Evanston, IL. 2003. Web. 1 July 2010. Conference paper.

Debray, Regis. *Transmitting Culture*. New York: Columbia UP, 2000.

DeLanda, Manuel. *New Philosophy of Society: Assemblage Theory and Social Complexity*. New York: Continuum, 2006.

Deleuze, Gilles, and Félix Guattari. *A Thousand Plateaus: Capitalism and Schizophrenia*. Trans. Brian Massumi. 1980. Minneapolis: University of Minneapolis Press, 2005.

———. *Kafka: Toward a Minor Literature*. Trans. Dana Polan. Minneapolis: University of Minnesota, 1986.

Deleuze, Gilles. *Difference and Repetition*. 1968. Trans. Paul Patton. New York: Columbia UP, 1994.

Dosse, François. *Gilles Deleuze and Félix Guattari: Intersecting Lives*. Trans. Deborah Glassman. New York: Columbia UP, 2010.

Douglass, Frederick. *Narrative of the Life of Frederick Douglass, an American Slave*. 1845. Berkeley Digital Library SunSITE. UC Berkeley, 14 May 1997. Web. 20 July 2011.

Edbauer, Jenny. "Unframing Models of Public Distribution: From Rhetorical Situation to Rhetorical Ecologies." *Rhetoric Society Quarterly* 35.4 (2005): 5–24.

Eden, Kathy. *Hermeneutics and the Rhetorical Tradition: Chapters in the Ancient Legacy and Its Humanist Reception*. New Haven: Yale UP, 1997.

Emirbayer, Mustafa, and Ann Mische. "What Is Agency?" *American Journal of Sociology* 103.4 (1988): 962–1022. JSTOR. Web. 17 April 2012.

Fackenheim, E. *Metaphysics and Historicity*. Milwaukee: Marquette UP, 1961.

Farrell, Thomas. *Norms of Rhetorical Culture*. New Haven: Yale UP, 1993.

Fitch, Suzanne Pullon, and Roseann M. Mandziuk. *Sojourner Truth as Orator: Wit, Story, and Song*. Westport: Greenwood, 1997.

Foss, Sonja K., William J. C. Waters, and Bernard J. Armada. "Toward a Theory of Agentic Orientation: Rhetoric and Agency in Run Lola Run." *Communication Theory* 17 (2007): 205–230.

Gardner, Christine J. *Making Abstinence Sexy: The Rhetoric of Evangelical Abstinence Campaigns*. Berkeley: UC Press, 2001.

Gordon, Lewis R. "African-American Philosophy, Race, and the Geography of Reason." *Not Only the Master's Tools: African American Studies in Theory and Practice*. Ed. Lewis R. Gordon and Jane Anna Gordon. Boulder: Paradigm, 2006. 3–51.

Gothlin, Eva. "Reading Simone de Beauvoir with Martin Heidegger." Card 45–65.

Grassi, Ernesto. *Rhetoric as Philosophy: The Humanist Tradition.* Trans. John Michael Krois and Azizeh Azodi. Carbondale: Southern Illinois UP, 2001.

Greene, Ronald Walter. "Another Materialist Rhetoric." *Critical Studies in Mass Communication* 15 (1998): 21–41.

———. "Rhetorical Materialism: The Rhetorical Subject and the General Intellect." Biesecker and Lucaites 43–65.

Grimson, Alejandro. "Culture and Identity: Two Different Notions." *Social Identities* 16.1 (2010): 61–77. Informaworld. Web. 14 Aug 2011.

Grondin, Jean. *Introduction to Philosophical Hermeneutics.* Trans. Joel Weinsheimer. New Haven: Yale UP, 1994.

Grøn, Arne, Iben Damgaard, and Søren Overgaard, eds. *Subjectivity and Transcendence.* Tuebingen: Mohr Siebeck, 2007.

Guattari, Félix. *Molecular Revolution: Psychiatry and Politics.* Trans. Rosemary Sheed. Harmondsworth: Peregrine, 1984.

Gusdorf, Georges. *Speaking (La Parole).* Trans. Paul T. Brockelman. Evanston: Northwestern UP, 1965.

Hall, Donald E. *Subjectivity.* New York: Routledge, 2004.

Hansen, Andrew C. "Dimensions of Agency in Lincoln's Second Inaugural Address." *Philosophy and Rhetoric* 37.3 (2004): 223–254.

Harman, Graham. *Heidegger Explained: From Phenomenon to Thing.* Chicago: Open Court, 2007.

Heidegger, Martin. *Poetry, Language, Thought.* 1971. Trans. Albert Hofstadter. New York: HarperCollins, 2001.

Heidegger, Martin. *"The Question Concerning Technology" and Other Essays.* 1954. Trans. William Lovitt. New York: Harper, 1977. 3–35.

Henry, Michel. *Material Phenomenology.* Trans. Scott Davidson. New York: Fordham UP, 2008.

———. *Philosophy and Phenomenology of the Body.* Trans. Girard Etzkorn. The Hague: Martinus Nijhoff, 1975.

Herndl, Carl G., and Adele Licona. "Shifting Agency: Agency, Kairos, and the Possibilities of Social Action." *Communicative Practices in Workplaces and the Professions: Cultural*

Perspectives on the Regulation of Discourse and Organizations. Eds. Mark and Charlotte Thralls. Amityville: Baywood, 2007. 133–153.

Hodges, Graham Russell Gao. *David Ruggles: A Radical Black Abolitionist and the Underground Railroad in New York City*. Chapel Hill: U of North Carolina P, 2010.

Hyde, Michael J. "The Call of Conscience: Heidegger and the Question of Rhetoric." *Philosophy and Rhetoric* 27.4 (1994): 374–396.

Johnson, Steven. *Interface Culture: How Technology Transforms the Way We Create and Communicate*. New York: Basic Books, 1997.

Kephart, John M., and Steven F. Rafferty. "Yes We Can: Rhizomic Rhetorical Agency in Hyper-Modern Campaign Ecologies." *Argumentation and Advocacy* 46. (2009): 6–20.

King, Wilma. *Essence of Liberty: Free Black Women During the Slave Era*. Columbia: U Missouri Press, 2006.

Kirkwood, Roxanne. "Liminal Spaces in Popular Culture: Social Change Through Rhetorical Agency." Diss. Texas Woman's University, 2005. Proquest. Web. 19 March 2009.

Koger, Larry. *Black Slaveowners: Free Black Slave Masters in South Carolina, 1790–1860*. Columbia: U of South Carolina P, 1995.

Kolata, Gina. "A Mystery Unraveled, Twice." *The New York Times*. 14 April 1998. F1, F6.

Kuhn, Thomas S. *The Road Since Structure: Philosophical Essays, 1970–1993*. Ed. James Conant and John Haugeland. Chicago: U of Chicago Press, 2000.

Lapansky, Phillip. "Graphic Discord: Abolitionist and Antiabolitionist Images." Yellen and Van Horne 201–230.

Latour, Bruno. *Pandora's Hope: Essays on the Reality of Science Studies*. Cambridge: Harvard UP, 1999.

———. *Reassembling the Social: An Introduction to Actor–Network Theory*. New York: Oxford, 2007.

———. *What Is the Style of Matters of Concern? Two Lectures in Empirical Philosophy*. Amsterdam: Van Gorcum, 2008.

Law, John. "Actor Network Theory and Material Semiotics." *The New Blackwell Companion to Social Theory*. Ed. Bryan S. Turner. Malden: Blackwell, 2009. 141–158.

Lee, Nick, and Paul Stenner. "Who Pays? Can We Pay Them Back?" *Actor Network Theory and After*. ed. John Law and John Hassard. Malden: Blackwell, 1999. 90–112.

Leff, Michael. "Tradition and Agency in Humanistic Rhetoric." *Philosophy and Rhetoric* 36 (2003): 135–147.

Lerner, Gerda. *The Female Experience: An American Documentary*. New York: Oxford UP, 1977.

Lévinas, Emmanuel. *Totality and Infinity: An Essay on Exteriority*. 1961. Trans. Alfonso Lingis. Boston: Martinus Nijhof, 1979.

Livesey, Graham. "Assemblage." Paar 18–19.

Lodge, Rupert Clendon. T*he Philosophy of Plato. 1956*. London: Routledge, 2000.

Lundberg, Christian O. "On Missed Encounters: Lacan and the Materiality of Rhetoric." Biesecker and Lucaites 161–183.

Lundberg, Christian, and Joshua Gunn. "'Ouija Board, Are There Any Communications?' Agency, Ontotheology, and the Death of the Humanist Subject, or, Continuing the ARS Conversation." *Rhetoric Society Quarterly* 35.4 (2005): 83–105.

Lunsford., Andrea, Kirt H. Wilson, and Rosa A. Eberly, eds. *The Sage Handbook of Rhetorical Studies*. Thousand Oaks: Sage, 2009.

Marcus, George E., and Erkan Saka. "Assemblage." *Theory, Culture, and Society*: 23.2–3 (2006): 101–109.

McGee, Michael Calvin. "A Materialist's Conception of Rhetoric." 1982. Biesecker and Lucaites 17–42.

McLuhan, Marshall. *Understanding Media: The Extensions of Man*. 1964. Cambridge: MIT Press, 1994.

McLuhan, Marshall, and Eric McLuhan. *Laws of Media: The New Science*. Toronto: U of Toronto Press, 1992.

McNeill, William. *The Glance of the Eye: Heidegger, Aristotle, and the Ends of Theory*. Albany: State University of New York Press, 1999.

Meillassoux, Quentin. *After Finitude: An Essay on the Necessity of Contingency*. Trans. Ray Brassier. New York: Continuum, 2008.

Miller, Carolyn R. "What Can Automation Tell Us About Agency?" *Rhetoric Society Quarterly* 37 (2007): 137–157.

Mol, Annemarie. *The Body Multiple: Ontology in Medical Practice*. Durham: Duke UP, 2002.
———. "Ontological Politics: A Word and Some Questions." *Actor Network and After*. Eds. John Law and John Hassard, eds. Malden: Blackwell, 1999. 74–89.
Nietzsche, Friedrich "On Truth and Lying in a Non-Moral Sense." *The Birth of Tragedy and Other Writings*. Cambridge: Cambridge UP, 1999.
O'Connor, Flannery. "Good Country People." *"A Good Man Is Hard to Find" and Other Stories*. 1955. Orlando: Harcourt Brace Jovanovich, 1977. 177–206.
Parr, Adrian, ed. *The Deleuze Dictionary: Revised Edition*. Edinburgh: Edinburgh UP, 2010.
Painter, Nell Irvin. "Difference, Slavery, and Memory: Sojourner Truth in Feminist Abolitionism." Yellin and Van Horne 139–158.
———. *Sojourner Truth: A Life, a Symbol*. New York: W.W. Norton, 1996.
Palmås, Karl. "Deleuze and DeLanda: A New Ontology, A New Political Economy?" Economic Sociology Seminar Series. Department of Sociology, London School of School of Economics and Political Science, 29 Jan. 2007. Web. 29 May 2010. Conference paper.
Perelman, Chaim, and L. Olbrechts-Tyteca. *The New Rhetoric: A Treatise on Argumentation*. Trans. John Wilkinson and Purcell Weaver. 1958. Notre Dame: U of Notre Dame P, 1971.
Phillips, John. "Agencement/Assemblage." *Theory, Culture, and Society* 23.2–3 (2006): 108–9.
Pisters, Patricia, and Wim Staat. *Shooting the Family: Transnational Media and Intercultural Values*. Amsterdam: Amsterdam UP, 2005.
Plato. *Phaedrus*. Trans. Alexander Nehamas and Paul Woodruff. Indianapolis: Hackett, 1995.
Ricoeur, Paul. *Freud and Philosophy*. Trans. Denis Savage. New Haven: Yale UP, 1970.
Rickert, Thomas. *Ambient Rhetoric: The Attunements of Rhetorical Being*. Pittsburgh: U of Pittsburgh P, 2013.

Sartre, Jean-Paul. *The Transcendence of the Ego: An Existentialist Theory of Consciousness*. Trans. and ed. Forrest Williams and Robert Kirkpatrick. 1937. New York: Hill and Wang, 1991.

Scarry, Elaine. *The Body in Pain: The Making and Unmaking of the World*. New York: Oxford, 1985.

Schrag, Calvin O. *The Self After Postmodernity*. New Haven: Yale UP, 1997.

Serres, Michel. *Angels: A Modern Myth*. Trans. Francis Cowper. New York: Flammarion, 1995.

Sheridan, David M., Jim Ridolfo, and Anthony J. Michel. *The Available Means of Persuasion: Mapping a Theory and Pedagogy of Multimodal Public Rhetoric*. Anderson, SC: Parlor Press, 2012.

Spinuzzi, Clay. *Network: Theorizing Knowledge Work in Telecommunications*. New York: Cambridge University Press, 2008.

Spivak, Gayatri Chakravorty. "Can the Subaltern Speak?" *Marxism and the Interpretation of Culture*. Eds. Cary Nelson and Lawrence Grossberg. Urbana: U of Illinois P, 1988.

Srnicek, Nick. (2007). *Assemblage Theory, Complexity and Contentious Politics: The Political Ontology of Gilles Deleuze*. Unpublished master's thesis, University of Western Ontario.

Stormer, Nathan. "Encomium of Helen's Body: A Will to Matter." Biesecker and Lucaites 215–227.

Strate, Lance. "Studying Media As Media: McLuhan and the Media Ecology Approach." *MediaTropes* 1 (2008): 127–142. Web. 3 March 2011.

Strathern, Margaret. *Partial Connections*. 1991. Walnut Creek: Rowman and Littlefield, 2004.

Thomas, Francis-Noël, and Mark Turner. *Clear and Simple as the Truth: Writing Classic Prose*. Princeton: Princeton UP, 1994.

Thomson, Iain. "Ontotheology? Understanding Heidegger's *Destruktion* of Metaphysics." *International Journal of Philosophical* Studies 8.3 (2000): 297–327.

Trapani, William C. "Materiality's Time: Rethinking the Event from the Derridean esprit d'à–propos." Biesecker and Lucaites 321–345.

Turnbull, Nick. "Rhetorical Agency as a Property of Questioning." *Philosophy and Rhetoric* 37.3 (2004): 207–222.

Venet, Wendy Hamand. *Neither Ballots Nor Bullets: Women Abolitionists and the Civil War.* Charlottesville: UP of Virginia, 1991.

Venn, Couze. "Cultural Theory and Its Futures: Introduction." *Theory, Culture, and Society* 24(3): 49–54.

Villadsen, Lisa Storm. "Speaking on Behalf of Others: Rhetorical Agency and Epideictic Functions in Official Apologies." *Rhetoric Society Quarterly* 38.1 (2008): 25–45.

Wallace, Karl R. "The Substance of Rhetoric: Good Reasons." *Quarterly Journal of Speech* 49.3 (1963): 239–49.

Weaver, Richard. "Language Is Sermonic." 1970. *The Rhetoric of Western Thought.* Ed. James L. Golden, Goodwin F. Bergquist, and William E. Coleman. 4th ed. Dubuque: Kendall Hunt, 1984. 304–317.

———. "The Phaedrus and the Nature of Rhetoric." *The Ethics of Rhetoric.* 1953. Davis: Hermagoras Press, 1985.

Webmoor, Timothy. "Dispelling Representation: Mediation as Practice." *Reconfiguring the Archaeological Sensibility: Mediating Heritage at Teotihuacan, Mexico.* Stanford University. 2007. Web 9 Sept. 2011.

"Welcome to the True Patriot Network." *True Patriot Network.* 2008. N.. pag. Web. 8 Feb 2012.

Werder, Carmen. "Rhetorical Agency: Seeing the Ethics of It All." *Writing Program Adminstration* 24.1–2 (2000): 7–26.

Williams, Forrest, and Robert Kirkpatrick. "Translators' Introduction." Sartre 11–27.

Williams, James. "Gilles Deleuze and Michel Henry: Critical Contrasts in the Deduction of Life as Transcendental." *Sophia* 47 (2008): 265–279.

Wise, J. Macgregor. "Assemblage." *Gilles Deleuze: Key Concepts.* Ed. Charles J. Stivale Montreal: McGill-Queen's University Press, 2005. 77–87.

Wyatt-Brown, Bertram. "American Abolitionism and Religion." *TeacherServe.* National Humanities Center, March 2008. Web. 3 March 2011.

Yellin, Jean Fagan and John C. Van Horne, eds. *The Abolitionist Sisterhood: Women's Political Culture in Antebellum America*. Ithaca: Cornell UP, 1994. 1–19.

Young, Amanda. "Disciplinary Rhetorics, Rhetorical Agency, and the Construction of Voice." *Rhetoric in Detail: Discourse Analyses of Rhetorical Talk and Text*. Eds. Barbara Johnstone and Christopher Eisenhart. New York: John Benjamins, 2008. 227–246.

Zahavi, Dan. "Subjectivity and Immanence in Michel Henry." Grøn, Damgaard, and Overgaard 133–148.

www.ingramcontent.com/pod-product-compliance
Lightning Source LLC
Chambersburg PA
CBHW072043160426
43197CB00014B/2615